THE HOLY SPIRIT

HIS GIFTS AND POWER ARE FOR YOU

DR. EUGENE G. GIVENS

Unless otherwise indicated, all scripture references are taken from the King James, New King James, or Amplified Versions of the Bible

The Holy Spirit: His Gifts and Power Are For You

ISBN: 978-0-9834128-0-9

Library of Congress Control Number: 2011903712

Printed in the United States of America.

Dr. Eugene G. Givens

DrEugeneGivens@hotmail.com

For additional copies of this book, go to:
www.booksofvalue.com

ABOUT THIS BOOK

From the early time period of the Old Testament, throughout the time period of the life and ministry of Jesus Christ, continuing through the time period of the Early Church, and throughout the world today, mankind has always had a thirst and hunger for supernatural ability, supernatural power, supernatural knowledge, and miracles. Even today, millions of dollars are spent throughout the world in pursuit of these desires.

In this book Dr. Givens, in a detailed, easy to understand and interesting way, reveals, documents, and explains *the manner* by which supernatural ability and power *of the Highest* has been made available to mankind throughout history. This supernatural power and ability *all* comes through the Holy Spirit of God, His Power, His Gifts; and they are available *for you* today. We will discover what the Gifts are, what they do, and see how they operate. We will understand how the Holy Spirit manifests Himself through the Inward Witness, and through His nine spiritual Gifts. We will understand *His purposes* for using us, and the *motives* we should have for Him to operate His Gifts *through us*, just as He has done through countless others throughout history *and still does today*.

We will behold the Master Connection between the Holy Spirit, His Power, and His supernatural Gifts. We will see the secret and vital importance of worship, and its association with the Gifts of the Spirit. We will discover what *the power* of the Holy Spirit is and how *we* can cause it to be released. From the Discerning of spirits we will discover *the reality of the spirit realm*, and the powers that affect the beings and activities of that realm. We will relish several *special assignments* given to the Author where spectacular activity by the Holy Spirit was displayed.

The chapter on Supernatural Deception is fascinating and extremely important. We'll identify demonic false and lying supernatural signs and wonders, and expose the methods and purpose of their use. We will learn from a scriptural passage *how to tell the difference* between the *true* supernatural signs, wonders, and miracles from the Holy Spirit of God, as compared to demonic and false supernatural activities from satanic evil powers that are dangerous and designed to *deceive* people. Finally, we will learn what essential steps *we* can take to *put ourselves* into position to be used by the Holy Spirit, His supernatural Gifts, His Power, and understand *why* we need them *now.*

There have been many books written about the Holy Spirit. But *this* book is about His *spiritual* Gifts and His Power. It is loaded with information that you will enjoy and be glad to know. It *is not* written as a result of the Author's own imagination, desire, or ability. It *is not* based upon *any* denomination, *nor* non-denomination, doctrine, influence, or preference. It *is* written based upon the Word of God, as a result of continuous prayer, and with directions and guidance from the Holy Spirit. **Get ready to be blessed, and get ready for a fascinating and exciting reading experience!**

ACKNOWLEDGEMENTS

It would be unthinkable for me not to acknowledge my appreciation to the key people who have made major contributions to me in the writing of this book. A little more than two years ago, three Godly men, all familiar with this ministry but none of whom know each other, spoke to me separately and at different times over a period of three months, and stated, "You ought to write a book!"

These men, in the order that they spoke to me, are the Rev. Elder Oscar Otis Owens, Jr., Los Angeles, CA., Mr. Royal Ailes, Broken Arrow, OK., and Mr. Calvan Nathan, Miami, Fla.; all three are devout Believers and have been long time friends of mine for more than twenty-five years. They unknowingly confirmed what the Holy Spirit had instructed me to do. With months of prolonged and continuous prayer, the subjects, contents, and guidance for writing this book were given to me by the Holy Spirit.

I also express my appreciation to Mr. Gerald Gioia, Lake Ridge, Va., who has been invaluable in helping me with the computer technology required in writing this book.

My profound appreciation goes to my long time associate and personal friend, Pastor Elbert L. Maxwell, Upper Montclair, N.J., for his diligent scriptural analysis and appropriateness as applied to certain subjects of this book, and especially to another personal friend, Pastor Willie Young, Gahanna, OH., who did an exhaustive editorial review of all material, designed the cover, and prepared this book for its publication. Their contributions are immeasurable.

With all modesty I extend my greatest and deepest appreciation to my wife, Mrs. Faye Rebecca Banks Givens, for the vital contributions she has given to me in writing this book. Her profound understanding and experience in ministering with the Gifts of the Holy Spirit, her spiritual insight, and her keenness to give caution of my secular forms of expression have proven to be invaluable. Her collaboration, counseling, and relevant editing have been indispensable. Quite bluntly, she is a phenomenal blessing. I thank God for her with all of my heart.

Dr. Eugene G. Givens

ABOUT THE AUTHOR

By profession, Dr. Eugene G. Givens became a practitioner of General and Reconstructive Dentistry. He holds a Bachelor of Arts degree from the University of Connecticut, a Master of Professional Services degree from the School of Health and Public Services at Long Island University, and a Doctor of Dental Surgery degree from the School of Dentistry at Temple University. He was commissioned as a U.S. Army Infantry Officer, and served as the Dental Surgeon of the First Armored Division during the Viet Nam era.

Dr. Givens has held faculty appointments at the University of Miami School of Medicine, the State University of New York School of Dental Medicine, and the former School of Dentistry at Oral Roberts University. He has taught, engaged in research, published scientific professional literature, and engaged in the private practice of dentistry. Dr. Givens has held licenses to practice clinical dentistry in eight states including New York, Florida, California, and Virginia.

By calling, and as an ordained minister, Dr. Givens is engaged in what he considers to be the highest blessing and activity of all human endeavors: the ministry of the Gospel of the Lord Jesus Christ. Forgetting those things which are behind, he presses towards the high calling of God in Christ Jesus; teaching and preaching the Gospel of Jesus Christ by the anointing of the Holy Spirit, His Gifts and power. He has experienced that the Gospel of Jesus Christ, through the inspired Word of God, is always confirmed with supernatural signs, wonders, and miracles.

His sole mission now is to glorify the Lord Jesus Christ, demonstrate the Kingdom of God, bring people into the Body of Christ through Salvation and the Baptism with the Holy Spirit, and with other Five Fold Ministry Gifts, build up the Body of Christ for the work of the ministry.

TABLE OF CONTENTS

INTRODUCTION

If you do not believe in God or the Lord Jesus Christ, you are going to discover things that cannot be disproven which will "blow your mind." If you are a *regular* Believer[A] with little knowledge and understanding of the Holy Spirit, His Gifts and His Power, you are going to discover a new dimension of spiritual insight, power, and activity. If you are a minister, the head of any church, denomination, or organization that embraces the Lord Jesus Christ, you will discover *major* Gifts that God has for you to bless His people and to help you fulfill His ministry through you. This book concerns the highest level of supernatural ability and power available to mankind, *and it is for you*. Keep reading!

How would you like to have access to *supernatural* activity which leads you into blessings, and enables you to avoid disaster? That activity is called, "Leading by the Holy Spirit through the Inward Witness." How would you like to have something revealed to you from God regarding facts or events that *occurred* in the past, or that *are occurring* at the present time that you did not know? That's called the Word of Knowledge manifested by the Holy Spirit. The Holy Spirit can also enable you to receive information from God pertaining to something that *will occur* in the future. That's called the Word of Wisdom.

In addition, the Holy Spirit can give you the ability to actually see into another dimension, called the spirit realm, where you can see angels and other spirit beings that surround us in that invisible realm. That's called the Discerning of spirits. Likewise, you can be given supernatural faith to

---

[A] **A Believer is someone who has received the Lord Jesus Christ as his, or her, personal Savior. Acts 2:21**

perform a phenomenal healing miracle. That's the Gift of Faith and The Working of Miracles operating together through the Holy Spirit.

Did you know that you can be used as a person or point of contact where people are healed, even without your knowledge? That can occur with the Gifts of Healings manifested by the sovereign will of the Holy Spirit. What many people are also unaware of is that, due to the ability to operate by the Holy Spirit in what are called the Gifts of Divine Vocal Communication, it is also possible to hear the voice of God, or speak to Him *yourself* in a Divine language that only *He* understands.

These are all functions of the Holy Spirit through what are called the *spiritual* Gifts of the Spirit, and they are all supernatural Gifts. Multiple examples of activities associated with these Gifts are found in many Books throughout the Bible. Therefore, it seems astounding that so many Christians have very little knowledge and understanding of these glorious spiritual gifts, and the unsearchable spiritual riches of Christ that are available through them. If we are uninformed, frightened, suspicious, or hostile to God's supernatural Gifts and Power, we can be deprived of His tremendous blessings that they bring.

Any of these Gifts can operate *through you* by a Divine Being called the Holy Spirit of God. The Holy Spirit is available for *all*, and His supernatural Gifts can be available to you too, as *He wills*. The purpose of this book is to reveal the manner as to how the Holy Spirit, His Gifts, and His Power can operate in your life. This is exceedingly vital because of the times in which we are living, and the things that shall soon come to pass.

God's historical plan for mankind extends from eternity past, throughout this present time period, and into eternity future. His plan is revealed through the Word of

God and is both accurate and true. On the contrary, history from man's perspective is subject to *his own interpretation*; some of which is real, some of which is false, some of which is deliberately omitted, some of which is inaccurate, some of which is fictionalized, and some of which is purposefully distorted. But all of the predictions and prophecies of the Word of God, from the beginning to this present time, have historically proven to be accurate and true. Therefore, we can have confidence that if what the scriptures explain about the events and conditions related to the past and this present time period have proven to be true, the events and conditions scripturally predicted for the future shall also prove to be accurate and true. For this reason, the need and value of having the Holy Spirit and His Gifts operating through us will become self evident as you read this book.

With this in mind, we'll examine scriptural examples of the operations of the Holy Spirit and His Gifts from the Old Testament, the earthly life and ministry of Jesus Christ, the Early Church, and actual experiences from the life and ministry of the Author.

The examples of the Author's personal experiences are based upon more than twenty-five years of ministry where seven of the nine Gifts of the Spirit have been in operation, at various times, during this period of time *at the will* of the Holy Spirit. These experiences occurred while ministering as an ordained minister of the Gospel to church congregations, to people in public evangelistic meetings, as a regular Believer to people requiring individual ministry, as a professional treating patients in private practice settings, and as experiences in private life for personal blessings. The examples are given *only* as testimony to confirm that the Holy Spirit and His spiritual Gifts are just as active, practical, valuable, and needed today, as they have been throughout history.

We are going to see how through the Holy Spirit and His Gifts, regardless of who you are, you too can share in the unlimited power and love of the Supreme Being who has absolute and total supreme power and authority *over all things* in every realm that exists.

Regardless of your place in life or societal status, your education, age, sex, color, and regardless of where you live in this world, *this book is for you.* So get ready to discover some fascinating things that can bring you into an intimate relationship with God, and lead you into a life of excitement that you never dreamed was possible. Listen, God is able to do exceedingly and super-abundantly above all you can ask or think a*ccording to the Power* that *can work in you!* [1] That Power is the power of the Holy Spirit. [2]

Now, to speak of "Power in you" can be very easily misunderstood. Some may think it refers to power of human physical ability, mental ability, or both. It is neither. Rather, it refers to a Divine Person in the form of a spirit who can be in you, with you, and who has the ability to exercise unlimited supernatural knowledge and power *through you!*[3]

This Person is the Holy Spirit. He is not an "it," He is not "a power," He is not "a presence." He is a Divine Person with power whose presence can be made known. The Holy Spirit is the One who will be showcased in this book. He represents the highest level of supernatural ability, power, and truth, along with the Word of God, that is available to mankind. He is available for all of us, [4] and *we need Him now!* Let's go into a little more detail as to why.

Why we need the Holy Spirit, His Gifts and Power Now

We are presently living at a time where current events and Biblical prophecy are coinciding to usher in a new phase of history that the Bible calls, "The End Times."

The fact that institutions, the conduct of mankind, and environmental stability are undergoing evil, noticeable, and significant breakdown is plainly obvious. Political corruption has become entrenched. We see economic collapse resulting from unbridled corporate and business greed. Violence, wars and unrest between nations, along with racial and ethnic hatred are increasing. Famines, pestilences, and troubles are spreading. Catastrophic earthquakes, volcanic eruptions, massive pollution of the earth and oceans, disappearance of biological species, and worldwide environmental destruction are occurring in an unprecedented manner. Various forms of perpetual evil is evident on one hand, while spiritual deception, gross hypocrisy, giving heed to false doctrines, and religious systems having forms of Godliness while denying the power of God, is evident on the other hand.[5] In addition, certain historical events involving the nation of Israel have now come to pass during our current time period exactly as predicted by scripture. As a result of all these conditions, the information in this book is needful for us to know *now!*

According to scripture, these factors and conditions represent *the beginning of sorrows* characteristic of The End Times which must come to pass.[6] This chaos will become endemic and progressive throughout societies worldwide. These conditions and the upcoming events are thoroughly described throughout scriptural passages from the Old Testament, the teachings of Jesus Christ, throughout the New Testament, and especially in The Book of The Revelation.[7] Yet, *many are unaware* of the literal and spiritual significance of this time period. Those who are aware understand the vital necessity of having the help of the Holy Spirit along with His Power and His spiritual Gifts operating through us during these times. ***This is not a time for fear!*** But it is a time for Godly understanding, directions, and power. This is exactly what the Holy Spirit and His Gifts provide.

One of the major characteristics of this time period is *deception*. The more that spiritual and natural deception occurs, the more it will be exposed by the Holy Spirit and His Gifts to raise up a standard against the onslaught by *knowledgeable* Believers.[B][8] This is another reason we need the Holy Spirit, His Gifts, and His Power operating through us right now. On a *few* occasions you may read something in this book which *appears* to be repetitive. This is done deliberately because of the importance of the subject.

What we must *avoid* and what we must *embrace*

In our effort to obtain greater insight and deeper understanding of the Holy Spirit and His *spiritual* Gifts, let us at all cost avoid discord and strife. Certain areas that shall be covered may be considered controversial by some. Unfortunately, discord, controversy and strife are nothing new. Even the disciples of Jesus quarreled among themselves as to who among them was the greatest.[9] In the Early Church, leaders disputed over the doctrine of circumcision, [10] and the Apostles Paul and Barnabus had such a great contention over who should accompany them to revisit the churches where they had previously preached, that they actually departed one from another and went separate ways. [11]

Sadly, *even today* some dispute and fall into strife over denominations, order of services, baptisms, communions, healing, and tongues as well as the spiritual Gifts of the Holy Spirit. When scripture and the Holy Spirit confirm any

---

[B] **Carefully read the Chapter on "How to Identify Supernatural Deception."**

subject to be true in your heart, never argue about the issue with *anyone*. Turn it over to God and let *Him* deal with them about it, not you. Strife and discord must be avoided because strife is extremely dangerous, and God hates discord. [12]

It seems perplexing that anyone would embrace the present day operations and fullness of the Godhead, except for the Holy Spirit. It also seems somewhat contradictory to believe that *in the future* the Holy Spirit will resurrect Believers from the dead, yet disbelieve the operations of His spiritual Gifts that are occurring *at the present* time. Nonetheless, please understand that there are wonderful and sincere Believers, even overflowing with much of the fruit of the Spirit,[C] who because of their educational background, theological training, church traditions, or lack of knowledge and experience in certain spiritual areas, simply will not believe in the *spiritual Gifts* of the Holy Spirit, nor believe the things you will discover in this book. Some may even go to great lengths trying to justify their disbelief; **documentation with scriptural examples and actual experiences not withstanding. Most of them just don't know, *and don't know that they don't know!***

But God is aware of this! He knows how difficult it is to break the traditions of men that cause the commandments of God to be of no effect, and He knows that men teach *their own* commandments *for doctrines of God.* So just as Jesus prayed for the Church and the Holy Spirit was sent to us from God, the Apostle Paul prayed for the Church also. He prayed that we would receive a revelation of that same Holy Spirit whom Jesus had without measure. This would include the *spiritual* Gifts of the Spirit as well, because they cannot be separated from the Holy Spirit any more than a person's

---

[C] **The fruit of the Spirit is the work of the Holy Spirit to bring love, joy, peace, long suffering, gentleness, goodness, faith, meekness, and temperance into a Believer's life. See Gal 5:22,23**

conduct can be separated from that person. [13]

All of us are products of our environment and what we have been taught. If we haven't been taught about the Holy Spirit, nor have had spiritual experience with Him, how in the world can we know *anything* about His spiritual Gifts? Furthermore, if we have been taught, but taught negatively or incorrectly, it's easy to develop a hardened attitude until the Holy Spirit Himself opens our eyes to see, believe, and *accept what the scriptures have to say* about Him and His spiritual Gifts.

Regarding the Holy Spirit, never feel condemned or allow *anyone* to put you down because of what you *don't know* about Him and His spiritual Gifts. The Lord is probably more concerned about those who don't know, and who *don't want to know*.

Those of us in the Five Fold Ministry [D] have a special responsibility because we are the ones who are supposed to perfect the saints for the work of the ministry, and edify the Body of Christ until we all come into the unity of the faith. And to be honest, this is a particularly difficult task for pastors. They are responsible to insure *sound Biblical doctrines*, spiritual protection and care for those God has placed under their oversight.

Their congregations are often diverse in multiple ways and usually encompass a broad range of spiritual maturity. Pastors share in their people's joys and sorrows; their hopes, aspirations, and accomplishments, as well as the private and congregational milestones of their church. God is not the author of confusion, and confusion in their congregations regarding the Holy Spirit and His Gifts, is the

---

[D] The Five Fold Ministry is a Gift given to the Church by the Lord Jesus Christ. It is composed of Ministers of the Gospel called Apostles, Prophets, Evangelists, Pastors, and Teachers. They each have specific roles, and they are all suppose to work together to build up the Church; which is the Body of Christ. See Ephesians 4:8-13

last thing pastors need. Yet, for pastors too, the Holy Spirit and His Gifts are vital for edifying and perfecting the saints for the work of the ministry and grooming them to represent the Kingdom of God.

This book *uniquely presents* the Holy Spirit, His Gifts, and His Power *from a Christ-Centered perspective and is supported by massive scriptural documentation.* Those of us who have been blessed to have received knowledge and experience with the Holy Spirit, His Gifts, and His Power, must be willing to share what we have received with *all* ministers, saints, and even nonbelievers. This must be done with love, humility, and understanding, but on a sound scriptural basis without compromise. If we are Christ-centered, mature, and experienced with the Holy Spirit, His Gifts, and understand His purposes, we will know *by the Spirit* exactly how to bless and minister to pastors and their congregations the essential things of the Spirit without leaving confusion behind.

Scripture is the Word of God. It is true and it is magnified above all the Names of God. [14] Believe and put your trust in the Word of God before any tradition, church, or man, including the Author. **Make *the scriptures* from the Word of God found in the Holy Bible your *final authority*.** Pray, and study the listed supporting scriptures *for yourself.* You will find that in many instances, when you put all of the supporting scriptures together, they give additional insight and paint a broad picture of confirmation and understanding far greater than *the subject that is presented.* They also provide a wealth of information for teaching.

Ask the Holy Spirit to open the eyes of *your* understanding to receive from the scriptures what He wants *you* to know. The Holy Spirit is the One who will guide you into all truth. [15] God does not want us to have a lack of knowledge nor be ignorant of His spiritual Gifts. In fact, He knows that it is a lack of knowledge that causes His people to be destroyed. He will perfect that which concerns us. **Avoid** *strife* and *discord*, but **embrace** the *love of God, the scriptures*, and allow *peace* to rule in your heart as you read, discover, and discuss the wonderful information you're about to find in this book. [16] It is my prayer and expectation that through this book you will obtain greater insight, depth of knowledge, experience, and understanding of the Holy Spirit, His Gifts, His Power, His purposes, and through the Spirit, a marvelous revelation of the Lord Jesus Christ. **Let's go!**

Supporting Scriptures:
Introduction
Please read the scriptures

---

1 Eph 3:20, Rom 15:13, 2 Tim 1:7
2 Acts 1:8, 10:38, Rom 15:13, 1 Th 1:5
3 I Cor 2:9-11, Jn 14:17, 1Cor 3:16, Lk 10:19, Acts 4:33, Acts 1:8
4 Acts 10:38, Lk 11:13, Acts 4:31, Heb 4:12
5 2 Ti 3:1-5, 1Ti 4:1,2, Mt 15:6,7,8,18, Mt 24:37-38, Gen 6:5
6 Mt 24:6-8, Rev 6:4
7 Dan 2, 7, 12 Eze 37, 38, 39, 2 Ti 3:1-7, Mt 24:4-8, 21-24, Mt 24:7, 1 Ti 4:1, Rev 6:1-19:21
8 Jn 16:13, Is 59:19
9 Mk 9:33,34, Lk 9:46
10 Acts 15:1,2
11 Acts 15: 35-40
12 2 Ti 2:23-26, Jam 3:14-17, Prov 6:16,19
13 Mt 15:6-9, Jn 14:16,26, Eph 1:15-22
14 Ps 119:160, 138:2
15 Jn 16:13
16 2 Ti 3:16, 2 Ti 2:15, Hos 4:6, 1Cor 12:1, Ps 138:8, Col 3:14,15

CHAPTER ONE

THE HOLY SPIRIT

There is good understanding about the Lord Jesus Christ and rightly so. The same is true of God the Father. But the same is *not true* of the Holy Spirit. Yet, He represents one third of the Godhead, and is the most powerful force in existence. He is the Gift sent by God the Father to be *in* us and *with* us as a stand-by for Jesus to help us while we are here upon the Earth. [1] And He has *with* Him, His Gifts *and* His Power *for us!*

The Godhead consists of Almighty God, the Lord Jesus Christ, who is also called The Word of God, and the Holy Spirit. [2] The Holy Spirit, who is also God, [3] is a Divine Being called by many names. His names express the nature of His being, His character, and His work. So He is called the Spirit of God, the Spirit of Christ, the Holy Ghost, the Spirit of Might, the Spirit of Holiness, and the Spirit of Glory, just to mention a *few* of His names. [4] Everything God the Father and the Lord Jesus Christ does upon the Earth is done by the Person and Ministry of the Holy Spirit. It is essential that we learn of Him, and get to *know* Him.

Although the Person and works of the Holy Spirit are far too extensive to fully cover in this book, here are several essential things that we should know about Him.

As we learn of the Holy Spirit, we notice that He has *characteristics* common to a person. He speaks, He teaches, He hears, He searches, He has emotions, and He even can be grieved and quenched.[5] But He is *not* a *person* like us! He is Divine. On Earth, we are *confined* by time, space, and matter; whereas He is omnipresent and has the ability to be *any and everywhere* at any and all times. That's why He can be in you, in me, or in anyone else who will receive Him, *all* at the same time. We have *limited* wisdom, knowledge, and understanding; whereas He is omniscient and has *infinite* wisdom, knowledge and understanding of *all* things. We are *limited* in mental, physical and creative power and ability, whereas He is omnipotent. He has *infinite* power and ability; be it creative, mental, physical, or of any other type. We make mistakes; He doesn't. He is *infinitely* holy; we are not. His love is infinite; ours is a work in progress!

The Holy Spirit is the Power of God.[6] He *performs* words spoken by God, and brings order out of darkness and chaos. When God said, "Let there be light," by His own power the Holy Spirit caused light to be.[7] Through Jesus Christ, all things consist and Jesus upholds all things by the Word of His power.[8] The Power of Jesus is the Holy Spirit and the Word of God. Like glue, the Holy Spirit holds together the functions and existence of everything created; from the components of the smallest entity that exists, to the biological components of mankind, to the components of the universe and whatever lies beyond it.

Just as the Holy Spirit was instrumental in the creation of mankind, He was also instrumental in the birth of Jesus for life here upon the Earth through the process called the Incarnation. It is the Holy Spirit *who is used by the Father* to reveal to us who the Lord Jesus Christ is, and who draws us to Jesus for eternal salvation. Just as flesh begets someone born of flesh, a person's spirit can be regenerated, born anew, by the Holy Spirit. As the Holy Spirit raised Jesus from the dead, He will also raise those who belong to

Jesus from the dead. [9]

It is the Holy Spirit who joins us with Christ and the Father, and it is the Holy Spirit who empowers us for life and ministry to represent the Kingdom of God on Earth. The Holy Spirit seals us to be with the Lord Jesus Christ forever and enables us to live in love, in righteousness, and to overcome evil here upon the Earth. [10]

It is necessary to see how the Holy Spirit worked through the life and ministry of Jesus when He was here on Earth because that is exactly how He wants to work through us. Since He anointed Jesus for the work of *His* ministry, the Holy Spirit also wants to anoint us, infill us, dwell within us, and lead us *to do the same ministry works that Jesus did.* The Holy Spirit gives us "the fruit of the Spirit" to help form the character of Christ in us, and He gives us His magnificent "Gifts of the Spirit" to help us *to continue* doing the works of Christ. [11] See page 164, bold paragraph.

The Holy Spirit enforces obedience to words spoken by Jesus, and, to commands spoken in the Name of Jesus by Believers. When Jesus cast out devils that possessed people, it was the Holy Spirit who made it happen. When Jesus performed miracles to manifest His glory, it was the Holy Spirit who made it happen. When Jesus went about doing good, healing all who were oppressed by the devil, it was the Holy Spirit who made it all happen. [12]

It is vital that we have the Holy Spirit, His Gifts, and His Power working through us because He is the One who forms Christ in us to enable us to demonstrate, like Jesus did, the activities of the Kingdom of God; which true Believers will be privileged to do throughout all of eternity.[13] You're going to hear a lot about the Kingdom of God, but there is another kingdom called the kingdom of darkness that we *must* also know about. The Holy Spirit, His Power and His

Gifts, have a dramatic impact on *that* kingdom. The chapter on "Essential Steps to Take" gives a good overview of each kingdom.

Sometimes there are extremely difficult situations in life where we simply don't know what to do. If ever we needed true knowledge, wisdom, understanding, and counsel from God it is during such times as these. The Holy Spirit, also called the Spirit of the Lord, is the One who enables us to receive from God that true wisdom, understanding, counsel, and strength which we need at such times.[14] Given the difficult times in which we are living, it is good to know that the Holy Spirit and all of His wonderful attributes are available to help us. The Holy Spirit makes these wonderful blessings available to us *in addition* to His marvelous *spiritual* Gifts. Are you beginning to get the picture here, as to how *important* the Holy Spirit *really* is?

Although we cannot see the Holy Spirit, He has ways of expressing Himself to make Himself known to us. These expressions are called "manifestations" or "operations" of the Holy Spirit. Listen, we cannot see the wind, either! But *we can see the results of its power* when we see a tree that the wind has caused to fall. We can *feel its presence* from a gentle refreshing breeze. Neither can we see the Holy Spirit! But *we can see the results of His power* when we see blind eyes opened, a shortened leg grow out, or a tumor mass disappear during His Ministry.

We're going to concentrate on two methods of manifestations which are extremely important *for us*. They are called "the Inward Witness," and, the *spiritual* Gifts of the Holy Spirit which are commonly called "the Gifts of the Spirit." Both of these types of manifestations represent His Divine presence. But before we discuss either, it is important that we understand the manner in which the Holy

Spirit works with the Lord Jesus Christ on our behalf and on behalf of others. Understanding this relationship is also critical in understanding the operations of the Gifts of the Spirit.

Here's the process. All of the Godhead dwells bodily in Christ Jesus. Therefore everything God has, including His wisdom and knowledge, belongs to Jesus too. The Holy Spirit in us takes the things that belong to Jesus and *reveals them to us* through *our* spirit. Our spirit takes the information it receives from the Holy Spirit, and communicates that information to our mind. Along with God's Word, this is how we have the mind of Christ. The Holy Spirit speaks to us what He hears from Jesus, just like Jesus spoke to people during His days on Earth the things He heard and saw by the *Spirit* from God the Father. Jesus, who is *the* Truth, calls the Holy Spirit the Spirit of Truth who can show us things to come. So it is the Holy Spirit who guides us into *all* truth pertaining to things which were, which are, and which are to come. [15]

Since the Holy Spirit communicates with both the Lord Jesus Christ and God the Father, He and His spiritual Gifts are linked up with the wisdom and knowledge of God the Father *and* the Lord Jesus Christ. In addition, the Holy Spirit searches *all* things, even the *deepest* things of God. He even searches things *hidden* in the darkness of evil that are beyond man's ability to know. [16] Therefore, He too has all knowledge and understanding. Wow! How great! This leads us to the primary role of the Holy Spirit in manifesting His Gifts today, and our purpose in being used by Him.

The Primary Role of the Holy Spirit in Manifesting His Gifts

The primary role of the Holy Spirit in manifesting His Gifts is to reveal and glorify the Lord Jesus Christ. [17]

This too, then, *must* be our purpose. It is during the process of having the Gifts of the Spirit working through us that the Lord Jesus Christ is revealed and glorified, the Kingdom of God is demonstrated, and people are blessed; *the greatest* of which occurs when someone receives the Lord Jesus Christ as their personal Savior. **Our *motive* for desiring to be used with the Gifts of the Spirit should be *only* to reveal and glorify the Lord Jesus Christ, demonstrate the Kingdom of God, and be a blessing to people.[18] Period.** That being the case, let's look at the components of our motive to see why they are so important.

To Reveal Jesus

When we talk about revealing Jesus we must understand that the Lord has always wanted to reveal Himself to the people He has created. He first revealed Himself to people of the Old Testament beginning with Adam. God revealed Himself to Moses visually, and by speaking to him. In the earthly life and ministry of the Lord Jesus Christ, God revealed Himself through the words that Jesus spoke and by the miracles Jesus did through the Holy Spirit. That's why Jesus told the people of His day that if they didn't believe and have a revelation of who He was, then to *believe the works* that He did. Even a ruler of the Jews named Nicodemus confessed that no man could do the miracles Jesus did, except that God be with him!

It's important to reveal Jesus so that all may know

that *He is God,* [19] and it is important to know that Jesus Christ is a revelation of God the Father. That's why Jesus said, "If you've seen me you have seen the Father." [20] It is through Jesus Christ, the Word of God, and the Holy Spirit, that God is revealed and we are enabled to know Him.

In the Early Church we see that Jesus revealed Himself to the Apostle Paul when, as Saul, he was on the way to a city called Damascus to persecute Believers. In the Book of the Hebrews, we see that the Believers in the Early Church clearly knew that God revealed Himself in various ways in times past by speaking through the prophets, and finally revealed Himself by speaking through His Son, Jesus Christ. Jesus reveals Himself today by speaking through the Holy Spirit, through the Gifts of the Spirit, and through the Word of God; which is the most trustworthy kind of revelation. [21] So *our first desire* should be to have the Holy Spirit reveal Jesus so that all may know that He is real, and that He is God. *Of all of the reasons for desiring to be used by the Holy Spirit and His Gifts, to have the Lord Jesus Christ revealed is the greatest.*

To Glorify Jesus

We see Jesus glorified when the Holy Spirit, by the Spirit of Glory, produces splendor, glory, and amazement as He manifests the Gifts of the Spirit and brings forth marvelous supernatural signs, wonders, and miracles. [22] *Jesus said the Holy Spirit would do this!* Since it's the desire of the Holy Spirit to do this, then it must be *our desire* to see the Holy Spirit glorify Jesus, too. Jesus *alone* is worthy of receiving *all* glory, honor and praise.

The glorification of the Lord Jesus Christ by the Holy Spirit should be of no surprise to us because it follows a pattern. Jesus glorified God by the Holy Spirit. Since Jesus and God are one, when the Holy Spirit *uses us* to glorify Jesus, He is also using us to glorify God. *Everything* God has created is for His pleasure and glory. The whole universe, with its majestic galaxies and stars is for His glory. The brilliant sun, the moon, the majestic ranges of snow capped mountains and deep lush valleys, all display His glory. The Earth and the seas, and all of the fullness thereof, are created for His pleasure and glory. He created all things, and they were and are, created for His pleasure. [23] That's why it's important that we glorify Him.

We, the people God has created, are the crown jewels of His glory; for we are created in His image, and created to love and have fellowship with Him through Jesus Christ. The Gifts of the Spirit are for the glory of Jesus. It is the Holy Spirit who *enables* us to glorify Him through the Gifts, to reveal Him, and to do that which we have been mainly created to do: Love God, and have fellowship with Him. [24]

To Demonstrate the Kingdom of God

When we talk about demonstrating the Kingdom of God, we must understand that God *has always had* a Kingdom. All that God is and all of His resources are in His Kingdom. Jesus revealed and demonstrated that Kingdom with all of its love, goodness, provisions, power, and glory. Now, through His Name and by His Spirit, Believers are also given the authority to access and demonstrate the Kingdom of God here on Earth. God wants *His will* to be done here upon the Earth as it is in Heaven. His will is for His Kingdom to be demonstrated here on the Earth, as it is in Heaven, *through us*. This is also part of the great commission Jesus

Christ has given to us because the Gospel is also related to the Kingdom of God. The Kingdom of God is wonderful. We who are in Christ are in it. It should be our desire to have the Holy Spirit, His Gifts and His Power demonstrate God's Kingdom through us *to others*.

To Be a Blessing to People

When the Holy Spirit manifests His Gifts through us to people, *they* are blessed. But the greatest blessing occurs when those who have not received Jesus Christ as their personal Savior, behold the revelation of Jesus in the presence of His glory, and submit to Him as Lord and Savior. According to scripture, *salvation* which was first spoken by the Lord, was then confirmed to those who heard, by God bearing witness to them with signs and wonders, and with diverse miracles, and gifts of the Holy Ghost; according to His own will. Here we see from scripture a clear connection between the Gifts of the Spirit and salvation. [25] Even the angels in Heaven rejoice when salvation occurs. [26] Scripture tells us many, many times, that people believed in Christ when they saw the miracles that He did. His miracles were performed by the Gifts of the Holy Spirit. This is important, so why not let the Holy Spirit *use you too*, to be a part of the salvation process using His Gifts? [27]

The Holy Spirit Confirms the Word of God

The way we get to know the Lord Jesus Christ, God the Father, the Holy Spirit, and *everything* pertaining to life and Godliness, is *through* the Word of God. The Word of God is so important that God magnifies His Word above all of His

Name. **But it is the Holy Spirit who reveals and causes us to understand that which is written in the Word, and to understand and know the Lord Jesus Christ, God the Father, and the Holy Spirit Himself**.

God knows there are, and always has been, satanic efforts made to corrupt His Word. So He has a way of illustrating the integrity and truth of His Word. The method He uses is to *confirm* His Word by the Holy Spirit with *supernatural* signs, wonders, and miracles. These all come through the Gifts of the Holy Spirit, who is the spirit of Truth. The Gifts of the Holy Spirit are the convincing proof the Lord uses to authenticate, firmly establish, endorse, validate, ratify and confirm His Word. They do not confirm or endorse *the person* He is working through. They confirm *God's Word!* Verifying the Word of God is an essential role of the Holy Spirit.[28]

Supporting Scriptures:
The Holy Spirit
Please read the scriptures

---

[1] Acts 2:38, Lk 24:49, Jn 16:7, Acts 1:4,5, Jn 14:16, 17, 1Cor 3:16, Rom 8:9

[2] 1Jn5:7, Jn 1:1

[3] Acts 5:3-4

[4] Gen 1:2, Acts 8:39, Rom 8:9, Rom 1:4, 1 Pet 4:14, Jn 1:33, 14:26, 16:13, Acts 10:38, 1Cor 6:19

[5] 2Sa 23:2, Acts 28:25, Jn 16:13, Acts 13:2, Jn 14:26, 1Cor 2:10, Eph 4:30, 1Th 5:19

[6] Acts 10:38

[7] Gen 1:2,3

[8] Heb 1:3, Col 1:17

[9] Job 33:4, Gen 1:26,27, Mt 1:18, Jn 3:3-8, Rom 8:11

[10] Mt 16:13-17, Jn 6:44, Jn 6:40, Jn 17:20-23, 1Cor12:13, Gal 6:6-9, 2 Pet 1:3, 1Cor 4:20, 1Cor2:4,5 Eph1:13,

Rom 8:2

[11] Acts 10:38, Mt 3:16, Rom 8:14, Gal 5:22-25, 1Cor 12:1-10, Jn 14:12, Mk 16:15-20, Mt 28: 18-20

[12] Mt 12:28, Lk 11:20, Jn 2:1-11, Acts 10:38

[13] Dan 7:27

[14] Isa 11:2

[15] Jn 16:15, Jn 16:13,14, Jn 14:17, 1 Cor 2:12-16

[16] 1 Cor 2:9-11, Dan 2:22

[17] Jn 16:14,

[18] 2 Th 1:11,12

[19] Jn 1:1, 14, Phil 2:5, 6, Mt 1:23-25

[20] Jn 10:30, 14:9

[21] Acts 9:1-5, 26:14-16, Heb 1:1-3, Jn 5:39

[22] Mt 9:8, 15:29-31, Lk 5:24-26

[23] Ps 19:1, Isa 43:7, Jn 17:4, 22, Rev 4:11

[24] Jn 17:4, 10:30, Ps 104:30, Rev 4:11, Isa 43:7, Gen 1:27, Col 1:16, Jn 4:23

[25] Heb 2:2-4

[26] Lk 15:10

[27] Jn 2:11,23

[28] 2 Cor 2:17, 4:2, Mk 16:20

Chapter Two

THE INWARD WITNESS

As previously stated, one of the ways in which the Holy Spirit manifests Himself to us is through what we call the Inward Witness. It is by the Inward Witness that He leads us, guides us, warns us, gives us directions, and even confirms things to us.

God has put a spirit into every person. [1] Although housed in a body, we have a spirit and soul. [2] So the Holy Spirit, who is a spirit, leads us through our spirit. He does not lead us through our body nor through our mind, but by the spirit that is within us. This kind of leading by the Holy Spirit is called "leading by the Inward Witness," or "leading by The Spirit." [3] You may have heard Believers say that "something on the inside" told them to do something which turned out to be great, or to do something which they later found out caused them to avoid serious trouble. That "something on the inside" was the Holy Spirit leading them by the Inward Witness. This occurs when a Believer's spirit agrees with the leading of the Holy Spirit that dwells within him, or her. It's often called a "hunch" when nonbelievers are led by *their* spirit. This is different from being led by the Holy Spirit.

When He leads us like this, our minds usually don't understand the reason why, nor the purpose. Later, when we see the results we understand. While driving, have you ever had "something inside you" alert you to slow down even though you didn't know why? Then moments later, a little further up the road, see a car running a stop sign which would have broad-sided your car had you *not* slowed down! That would be an example of a warning and leading given to you through the Inward Witness.

Now let's look at several examples of this type of activity found in the earthly life and ministry of Jesus, the Early Church, and the life and ministry of the Author. No examples can be given from the Old Testament because the Holy Spirit did not *dwell* within people during those days and consequently could not lead them through their spirit. Instead, He came upon them and spoke directly to them. [4] On the other hand, Jesus was full of the Holy Spirit and had the Holy Spirit without measure. Because of the prayer of Jesus to God, today's Believers can have the Holy Spirit *with* them and *in* them. [5] The same was true for Believers during the Early Church era. Being led by the Inward Witness is nothing new. Such leading occurred with Jesus, with Paul and others in the Early Church, and it can occur with you.

Inward Witness
Life and Ministry of Jesus Christ

One of the greatest examples in scripture showing the Holy Spirit leading Jesus by the Inward Witness occurred when the Holy Spirit led Jesus into the wilderness to be tempted of the devil! This is a short example, but it is extremely powerful and educational.

In the Gospels of Matthew and Luke the Word says, "Jesus was led of the Spirit." [1] God didn't speak to Him in a voice or give Him a vision telling Him to go. He was *led* by the Spirit through the Inward Witness. But notice this: in the book of Mark the scripture says that, "Jesus was *driven* by the Spirit into the wilderness." [2] We know He was led, but Mark lays it out and describes the manner as to *how* He was led. He was *driven!*

Here's what the Holy Spirit wants us to know: He *normally* leads in a very *gentle* way. However, on certain occasions when God deems the reason to be extremely important or requiring quick action, the leading of the Spirit by the Inward Witness can be so strong and so powerful that you may feel driven and compelled to act. Normally, when being led in this manner, you do not understand the reason or purpose for which you are being led. But the purpose is known to God, to Jesus, and to the Holy Spirit. However, after being obedient by yielding and following the Inward Witness, you will eventually understand the reason.

In this case, it was an essential test for Jesus to confront and overcome the temptations of Satan. Jesus not only overcame all of the temptations, but at the same time during the process, He also *showed us* how to put Satan in his place: use the Word of God against him. [3] You'll see some thrilling examples of this type of experience carried out elsewhere throughout this book.

Inward Witness
The Early Church

In the Book of the Acts of the Apostles, we see in astounding detail an event *beginning* with the Holy Spirit using the Inward Witness, and *concluding* by God amazingly electing to use an angel instead of the Holy Spirit to transmit some information to the Apostle Paul. This must have been extremely important to God because He sent His angel with the message directly to Paul himself, so that Paul would have no doubt. Here's the background.

Paul, an apostle of Jesus Christ, was despised by certain religious leaders of his day for giving testimony as to how he became a Believer of the Lord Jesus Christ. As a result, they rigged up phony charges against him to have the Roman authorities put him to death.[1] But because Paul was a Roman citizen, he demanded his right of citizenship to have his case heard by the Roman Emperor, Caesar. [2] So Paul and several other prisoners were placed under the guard of a Roman Centurion and put aboard a ship for the journey to Rome. [3]

However, the trip began very late in the sailing season. The weather was changing. The wind was getting bad. Winter was approaching and the weather continued to be in an upheaval. It was a very dangerous time for sailing. On the way, the weather became so bad that the initial ship carrying them docked as soon as it could and transferred those heading for Rome to another ship to continue the journey. [4] Now here's where the Holy Spirit enters upon the scene on behalf of Paul.

After considering all of the *circumstances* and *conditions*, Paul perceived grave danger ahead for the second part of the trip. Now get this! Paul not only went to the pilot who was responsible for the ship, and the Centurion who was responsible for his safety and that of the other prisoners, he even went to the owner of the ship; warning all three. This is what he said: "Sirs, I perceive that this voyage will be with hurt and much damage, not only to the laden and the ship, but also of our lives." The word, "laden" means cargo. They decided not to heed Paul's warning and sailed on anyway. However, the danger Paul perceived came to pass just as He had warned. [5]

Now how do we know this is the Holy Spirit leading Paul by the Inward Witness rather than the Holy Spirit manifesting one of the Gifts of the Spirit called the Word of Wisdom? In both cases, the *future* is involved. The answer lies in looking at the scripture to see what *it says,* and looking at the scripture to see what *Paul said* in the scripture.

Then we must look at the scripture to see what *it does not say*, and look at the scripture to see what *Paul does not say*. The *scripture says, Paul said, "I* perceive." In other words, Paul had a strong feeling inside, a strong impression, a grave apprehension, or profound inkling based upon the condition of the weather. These are all characteristic of leadings by the Inward Witness.

Scripture *does not say* the Spirit of God spoke to Paul or that God revealed to Paul in a vision or dream, what the danger was or what was going to happen in the future. Nor does *Paul say* in the scripture that the Spirit of God spoke to him, or that he had a vision or dream from God about the things that were going to happen. These are characteristic of a spiritual Gift called the Word of Wisdom.

When someone is spoken to by God through the Holy Spirit directly, or through a vision or dream from God, these activities are directed by the Holy Spirit Himself or by the Gifts of the Holy Spirit as we will see later. What Paul sensed is clearly an example of an advanced warning given to him through the Inward Witness based upon the conditions and circumstances *he perceived.* He believed that what he perceived was going to occur and told it in advance.

Later on, the danger Paul perceived actually did happen. In the midst of the storm God by-passed the Holy Spirit and sent an angel to tell Paul the extent of the danger and what the results would be.[6] This was direct action taken by God which Paul could not mistake.

Inward Witness
Life and Ministry of the Author

Unlike professors in regular colleges and universities, professors in medical and dental schools are usually required to be physically on site eight hours a day even if not engaged in teaching, clinical supervision of students, patient care, or research. Such was the case when I was on the faculty at a school of dentistry in the Southwest.

Early one afternoon while in my faculty office, the Spirit of God by the Inward Witness urged me to go home and pray. The urge became like a driving force. The issue for me became whether to stay until the required quitting time, or to obey the leading of the Spirit. I chose the latter.

After a hasty drive home I ran into the family room, dropped to my knees by the couch, and began fervently praying out of my own spirit, by the power of the Holy Spirit, in a language I didn't understand. After about twenty minutes of fervent prayer, I saw in a vision the head of a horse. Then I heard myself praying out loud, with great force in English, the protective verses of Psalm 91 over my daughter. After that, everything lifted and I no longer felt urged to pray or compelled to do anything. I do recall saying, "Lord, what in the world was that all about?" There was no answer.

My daughter, who played on the high school softball team, was due home about 5:30 P.M. following practice. When she still had not arrived by 7:00 P.M., I became somewhat concerned. Suddenly, she and her friend ran into the house with my daughter proclaiming, "I'm healed, I'm healed, by the stripes of Jesus I'm healed." When she moved her forearm from covering her mouth, I noticed a front tooth severely fractured. After asking what happened, she told me the following story.

After practice my daughter went home with one of her teammates, also her friend, who owned horses. She and her friend went horse back riding. The horse my daughter was riding ran down a hill, tripped, threw her off, and fell upon her! Can you imagine how dangerous that was and how catastrophic that could have been? Even though *I didn't know, the Holy Spirit knew* what evil was hidden in darkness to seriously harm my daughter. Thank God that by the Inward Witness, the Holy Spirit *compelled* me to go home and pray fervently in the Spirit for Divine protection over her. After hearing her story, I simply took her down to the Clinic and rendered the appropriate professional care she required for an injury that was relatively minor.

Never neglect to obey the leading of the Holy Spirit by the Inward Witness especially when you are urged to pray in the Spirit. You may never know *who* or *what* you are praying for, but it's always according to God's perfect will.[1] By the way, this demonstrates something else we should know: things good *and* bad originate in the spirit realm *before* they occur in this natural realm. Through prayer, we have the ability to help *bring forth* good things, and also *stop* evil things from occurring. Be sure to read the supporting scriptures given about this.[2] Now let's see an example as to how the Holy Spirit used the Inward Witness to accomplish the most important blessing of all: *eternal salvation.*

One evening the Holy Spirit impressed me to call an attorney in Miami, Florida whom I had known for more than twenty years. I inwardly knew that my reason for calling was to access his status regarding eternal salvation through Jesus Christ. He was surprised to hear from me, and even more so to learn that I had become a minister of the Gospel.

From our conservation, it became easy to discern that he may not have received Jesus as his personal Savior.

In fact, he stated that he had no idea whether he would go to Heaven or hell if he died. But, he found it amusing that in addition to me, two other men recently talked to him about eternal salvation.

The Holy Spirit then began to impress upon me the urgent need to see him quickly. I offered to fly down from Oklahoma, at my own expense, if he would consent to seeing me. He agreed to meet me two days later in his home about 7:30 P.M.

Two days later, I was picked up at the Miami airport by a longtime Christian friend. He offered me a place to stay and drove me to the attorney's home, which was about fifteen miles away. I called the lawyer to confirm our 7:30 P.M. appointment. Everything was on!

We arrived at the lawyer's home at the appointed time. He was not there. His wife whom I also knew, but hadn't seen in over fifteen years, was very hospitable and amazed that such an effort was being made to see her husband. At eight-thirty her husband still had not arrived. So she called him and was told that he got "caught up" in the office but would see us soon. Ten-thirty, then eleven-thirty came and went. There still was no arrival of the attorney and we were unable to make contact with him. My friend and I felt it inappropriate to stay any longer with his wife, but before leaving we inquired about her salvation. The bottom line is this: *She* received Jesus Christ as *her* personal Lord and Savior. I shall never forget her words: "Gene, you came down here to see my husband, but the Lord may have sent you here *for me!"*

A week or so later back in Oklahoma, I received a phone call from Miami. My friend, the lawyer who refused to see us, unexpectedly died. Despite the efforts made, I was very saddened to learn of this sudden loss of my friend. Just remember, the Holy Spirit will not lead you in error by the

Inward Witness. Now, let's look at a couple of ways the Holy Spirit uses the Inward Witness to benefit us for *our own personal* help.

The Inward Witness as Our Spiritual Helper

There is a function of the Holy Spirit that we hear little about. But it is valuable to us on a personal basis for spiritual as well as practical success. It is the role of the Holy Spirit as our individual Helper.

He helps us to be effective in the spirit realm by helping us to pray supernaturally when we don't know how to pray as we ought. [3] He has the ability to search the mind of Christ and the deep things of God to determine God's perfect will for us, and then help us to pray God's perfect will with moans, groans, and in languages *unknown* to us but which *are known* to God. This occurs when the Holy Spirit leads us by the Inward Witness to pray.

I am absolutely convinced that when we, through the leading of the Inward Witness, seek the Lord with all of our heart, the Holy Spirit will pray *through* us the perfect will of God for us. This may help perfect us in true righteousness, and help us to be an overcomer in the Kingdom of God in such a way as to even insure our reign with the Lord Jesus Christ throughout eternity. [4]

The Inward Witness as Our Natural Helper

The Holy Spirit can also help us *here upon the Earth* in very common and practical ways. Sometimes this help comes directly from the Holy Spirit Himself. At other times it comes from those He directs us to. Let me give you a couple of examples.

Several years ago, while performing a surgical procedure on a patient, I encountered a problem that was giving me great difficulty to solve. So I stepped aside for a moment and quietly prayed. I told the Holy Spirit that He knew all things, could do all things, knew this problem, and knew that I needed His help. I asked Him to help me. I then returned to the patient, picked up the exact same instrument and *began* to continue with the operation. *The problem resolved itself instantly!* Here's another example.

In the Springtime, the state of Virginia is saturated with beautiful green trees. However on certain days the level of pollen in the air can be extremely unhealthy. This was the case when I decided to cut the grass one day while my wife was out of the country. I desperately needed my face mask. Despite searching the house, I could not find the mask *anywhere*. So once again, I asked the Holy Spirit for help because I knew that He knew exactly where the mask was. Without thought, I found myself wandering into a room, opening a cabinet, and looking directly at the mask in the corner of a shelf. My wife had put it there before she left *without telling me*. Listen at this! The mask was in a place I would have *never* put it, nor looked for it *there*. This was definitely the action of the Holy Spirit leading me by the Inward witness to that specific place where the mask could be found. He can help you the same way!

Very recently, I was driving to visit our daughter when I made a wrong turn and was unable to reverse course. I ended up totally lost in an area where I had no sense of direction and was absolutely unfamiliar with. Traveling down a street I was impressed to make a right turn onto another unfamiliar street. Half way down the block I saw two women walking from a house to enter a car. I stopped to ask them for help with directions. The first lady deferred to the other, who proceeded telling me directions, then suddenly stopped and said, "Follow me. I'm going that way right now!"

What are the probabilities that being lost I would be led to turn down a particular street, encounter a stranger at that particular moment who would say follow me, I'll lead you to the exact location you are looking for because I'm going there, too? This is an example of the Holy Spirit leading by the Inward Witness to someone else who can provide help. Only the Holy Spirit can do this! Now let's look at an example as to how ignorance of the manifestation of the Inward Witness can be dangerous and tragic.

Ignorance of the Manifestation of the Inward Witness *can be Dangerous*

While in private practice in Miami, Florida, a patient presented herself to us for some advanced dental care. She was a wonderful, optimistic teacher who attended the same church that I did. Unlike her cheerful demeanor at previous office visits, on *this* occasion she was extremely forlorn and sad. She quietly sobbed with uncontrollable tears even before treatment was to begin, and she could not explain her emotional state. Unbeknown to us, the Holy Spirit was warning her of great impending danger to come. *At that time* neither she nor I had any *spiritual* understanding of the Holy Spirit, and we certainly knew nothing of His manifestations. Out of desperation I consoled her the best I knew how, and dismissed her without treatment. The next day, three of her close relatives lost their lives when their automobile was hit by a train! Were we not ignorant of the Holy Spirit and His manifestations, I am certain that that tragedy could have been averted by sufficient prayer in the Spirit. It can be dangerous and tragic to be uninformed about, or to ignore, the Inward Witness. Thank God *you* are being more informed.

So what can we learn from all of these examples? Well, first of all, the primary way the Holy Spirit leads us is by our spirit through the Inward Witness. This requires us to be open and sensitive to Him. When you have that sense of leading, perception, belief, caution, or a sense of need to act, tell the Holy Spirit about it *and ask* Him not to let you be *misled.* Then follow through *and act* on whatever you perceive He wants you to do, even if it seems very small! If you have a feeling of dread, or sense that something is wrong but you don't know what it is, pray fervently in the Spirit until you get a sense of peace and relief. The Holy Spirit will help you.

In private, commune with the Holy Spirit as often as you can.[5] It may appear to be a one way conversation, but *He hears you.* Notice, I said *in private!* If you commune with Him in public or around people, they'll think you're nuts. Don't go there!

Begin to pray and study the scriptures. Seek the Lord Jesus Christ with all of your heart. Increase your efforts at this, just like exercising, as time goes by. It won't happen overnight, but in time you will find yourself flowing with the Holy Spirit in greater accuracy, with more purpose, and with greater joy and excitement. Don't try to be *super spiritual.* Just be normal, but always have the Lord in the back of your mind. The Holy Spirit will do the rest and perfect that which concerns you in all areas. The Holy Spirit wants us to know that He can help us in very practical ways, *and* in spiritual situations. He is of immense value to us; let us also *greatly* value Him.

Now we will shift our full attention to the Supernatural

Gifts of the Holy Spirit. But there is a *master connection* between the Holy Spirit and His Supernatural Gifts which should be thoroughly understood first. Therefore, we're going to cover this Master Connection next.

Supporting Scriptures:
The Inward Witness
Please read the scriptures

---

[1] Zec 12:1
[2] I Th 5:23
[3] Rom 8:14
[4] I Sa 16:13, Judges 6:34, Num 11:25
[5] Jn 14: 16,17

Supporting Scriptures:
The Inward Witness
Life and Ministry of Jesus Christ
Please read the scriptures

---

[1] Mt 4:1, Lk 4:1
[2] Mk 1:12
[3] Mt 4:4,7,10

Supporting Scriptures:
Inward Witness
The Early Church
Please read the scriptures

---

[1] Acts 22:1-22, 23:12-14, 20,21
[2] Acts 22:25-27
[3] Acts 27:1,2
[4] Acts 27:4-6
[5] Acts 27:9-11
[6] Acts 27:23-25

Supporting Scriptures:
Inward Witness
Life and Ministry of the Author
Please read the scriptures

---

[1] 1Cor 14: 14, Rom 8:26,27
[2] 2 Ki 20:1-5, Eph 6:10-12,
[3] Rom 8:26,27, 1Cor 14:14, 15
[4] Rev 2:25-29, 3:21
[5] 2 Cor 13:14

CHAPTER THREE

THE MASTER CONNECTION

When it comes to the glorious Gifts of the Spirit, the Holy Spirit in all of His works always reveal the reality of the One who is omnipresent, omniscient, and omnipotent. [A] That "One" is the Lord Jesus Christ.

***The Master Connection* between the Holy Spirit and the manifestation of His Gifts *is the Lord Jesus Christ.* The Lord Jesus Christ is the center and the essence of all things pertaining to the Holy Spirit and the Gifts of the Spirit. The Gifts also symbolize and reveal Him. We can clearly see that Jesus is the Master Connection when we realize three things: first, the eternal *relationship* between Jesus and the Holy Spirit; secondly, a major *attribute* of Jesus displayed by the Holy Spirit; and thirdly, the manner in which the Holy Spirit *reveals and glorifies* Jesus *through* the Gifts of the Spirit.**

We shall also observe that there is a functional relationship between the Holy Spirit and the Spirit of Grace, the Spirit of Christ, and the Spirit of Glory. Then we shall see *how* the Lord Jesus Christ is revealed by the Holy Spirit *functioning as* the Spirit of Grace, the Spirit of Christ, and the Spirit of Glory when the Gifts are in manifestation. We will discover

---

[A] **The One who is present at all times in all places. The One who has total knowledge of all things: past, present, and future. The One who has Supreme power over all things, in all realms.**

that the Gifts enable magnificent results for both God and man. This is going to be an exciting and informative revelation. So it's a good time to pray and ask the Holy Spirit to make what you're going to read clear and understandable *to you.*

What we're going to discuss is absolutely *in no way* some kind of new doctrine. Nor is it intended to add to, or take away from the Word of God. It is a commentary given *only* to illustrate *the centrality of Christ* with the manifestation of the Gifts of the Spirit, just as He is the center piece elsewhere throughout the Bible from Genesis to The Revelation. With that in mind let's examine this Master Connection in greater detail.

Jesus Christ and the Holy Spirit

The Holy Spirit is the great *revealer.* He reveals and discloses Jesus to us in line with the Word of God *just like Jesus said He would do!* That's because the Word of God and Jesus are the same.[1] The Holy Spirit has always co-existed with Jesus. Like Jesus, He is a member of the Godhead and is therefore eternal.

Scripture tells us that the worlds were framed by the Word of God, that Jesus Christ laid the foundation of the Earth, and that the heavens are the works of His hands. But it is the Holy Spirit, who is also called the Spirit of Christ, who made it all happen. Notice that scripture also reveals the Holy Spirit as the Eternal Spirit, as well as the Spirit of Christ.[2] This shows the extensive, intimate, and perpetual relationship between the Lord Jesus Christ and the Holy Spirit. This relationship will last forever.

Jesus Christ and Grace

One of the major and pre-eminent *attributes* of Jesus displayed by the Holy Spirit is grace. Grace is the infinite goodness, compassion, mercy, kindness, and favor God has for us because of His inexhaustible love *for us*. Every good and perfect gift comes from Heaven.[3] The grace of God is His free gift *to all* who come to Him through Jesus Christ. God's grace is dispensed by the Holy Spirit.

Scripture tells us that there is a throne in Heaven. That throne is called the Throne of Grace. Sitting on that throne is the God of all Grace. At God's Right Hand is His Son Jesus Christ who is full of grace, and who is the giver of God's grace. Jesus ascended into Heaven to the Throne of Grace when He arose from the dead. He is there with God the Father and He communes with the Holy Spirit; who is also called the Spirit of Grace.

The Gospel is called the Gospel of Grace. Through this Gospel comes the Word of Grace that leads to salvation through Christ Jesus. By grace we are saved through faith, justified, and given right standing with God.[4] We can see that The Lord Jesus Christ *and grace* are inseparable.

This time period in which we are living is called the "dispensation of Grace." Therefore, by the Holy Spirit through prayer, we can come to the Throne of Grace where the God of Grace is. There we can obtain mercy and find grace from God to help us in our times of need. It seems that grace is extremely important![5] The question then is, "What has grace to do with the Gifts of the Holy Spirit?" As we shall see when we observe the Spirit of Grace, *everything*!

Jesus Christ and the Gifts of the Spirit

Seven of the nine Gifts of the Spirit were available to operate *with some* during the Old Testament era, and seven operated through Jesus Himself. All nine Gifts of the Holy Spirit are available to operate *through many* during this present era. Some Believers "major" exclusively on the Gifts of the Spirit. I love the Gifts of the Spirit, too. But here is the eye opening secret: The Holy Spirit represents the Lord Jesus Christ in all of the fullness of His love, His grace, and His supernatural Divine power *through* the Gifts of the Spirit.

It is so easy to get caught up in the excitement of the Gifts of the Spirit and the flare of some people through whom the Gifts operate, that we sometimes neglect to appreciate the value of their foundation; which is Jesus Christ. The Holy Spirit and His Gifts are connected to Jesus and the love and grace that Jesus has for us. Coming up in this chapter and going forth throughout this book, you will see the profound relationship and connection of Jesus Christ to the Holy Spirit and His Gifts.

Functions and *Revelations* of the Holy Spirit

The Holy Spirit is one spirit, *but He functions in different roles* and is often called by the name describing *what He does* in *that role* or *by who or what He reveals* in that role. We simply cannot get a thorough understanding and appreciation for the Gifts of the Spirit and their operations without understanding that it is Jesus who is revealed by the Holy Spirit when the Holy Spirit functions as the Spirit of Grace, as the Spirit of Christ, and as the Spirit of Glory; all of whom are revealed by the Holy Spirit as the Gifts of the

Spirit are manifested. This may sound a little complicated, so let's use an example of a hypothetical natural person to explain this spiritual principle in a simple manner.

Suppose there is a man named "Mr. Right" who flies a 747 Jumbo Jet, teaches aerodynamics at the local city college, and who owns a small hobby store where he sells model airplanes. When he flies, Mr. Right *is* a pilot, is *revealed* as a pilot, and *functions* as a pilot. When he teaches at the college, Mr. Right is a professor, *is revealed* as a professor, and *functions* as professor. When he operates his store, Mr. Right is a businessman, *is revealed as* a businessman, and *functions* as a businessman. Although Mr. Right is always the *same person* he is named and revealed according to the *role he is functioning in.* This same principle is true of the Holy Spirit.

A fine Biblical example of this principle, showing the Holy Spirit *called by* another name and functioning *in another* name *which reveals what He does*, is found in the life of Samson. In the Old Testament the Holy Spirit, also called the Spirit of the Lord, *functioned as* the Spirit of Might in the life of Samson; the strongman hero of the Bible. As the Spirit of Might, the Holy Spirit gave Samson mighty supernatural power, strength, and ability. This happened with Samson on multiple occasions. When he killed a young lion with his bare hands it was because he was enabled to do so by the Spirit of Might. When he slew a thousand men with the jawbone of a donkey, he was enabled by the Spirit of Might. When he slew thirty men that ambushed him early one morning, again, he was enabled to do so by the Holy Spirit *functioning* as the Spirit of Might. So here we see the Spirit of the Lord, who is the Holy Spirit, called the Spirit of Might when He functioned *as* the Spirit of Might to enable Samson to do extraordinary things using mighty supernatural power.[6]

By the way, the reason the Spirit of the Lord worked with Samson in such a fantastic way is that Samson, being a Nazarite, had a special relationship with God due to a special vow that he made to God. Today, those who believe in and who have received Jesus Christ as their personal Savior, have an even *better* relationship to the same God because of the Holy Spirit and a new special covenant with God. This new covenant was enabled by the Lord Jesus Christ and sealed with His Blood.

Now to continue, we see another example of this principle from the Old Testament which relates to the Holy Spirit in connection with Jesus Christ. The Prophet Isaiah lists seven Names of the Holy Spirit that would rest upon the Lord Jesus Christ: the spirit of the Lord, the spirit of wisdom and understanding, the spirit of counsel and might, the spirit of knowledge and of the fear of the Lord.[7] Since the Holy Spirit reveals and performs the things of God, the Spirit of the Lord functions to reveal the Lord. Likewise, the Holy Spirit *is called* the spirit of Might, and as the spirit of Might He functions to give supernatural strength, might, and ability. This same principle and ability of the Holy Spirit is true today. Therefore, let's now see this principle applied to the Holy Spirit functioning as the Spirit of Grace, the Spirit of the Lord Jesus Christ, the Spirit of Glory, and then see what the wonderful results are for God and for man.

The Holy Spirit and the Spirit of Grace, the Spirit of Christ, and the Spirit of Glory

The Gifts of the Spirit demonstrate the Holy Spirit functioning as the Spirit of Grace, the Spirit of Christ, and the Spirit of Glory; all of which reveal something about Jesus.

Jesus Christ is the One the Gifts *reveal*. Jesus is the One from whom *we receive* grace and benefits *through* the Gifts. Jesus is the One who *is glorified by* the Gifts. Functioning *as* the Spirit of Grace, the Spirit of Christ, and the Spirit of Glory, appears to be ways the Holy Spirit operates His Gifts. It appears that the reason *why* He operates His Gifts is so that He may continually *dispense to us* the grace of God, reveal Jesus, *glorify* Jesus, and *bring people* to Jesus.

God the Father, the Lord Jesus Christ, along with the Holy Spirit and His Gifts all work together in harmony for *our profit and benefit*. The *ultimate result* of the Holy Spirit manifesting His Gifts as the Spirit of Grace, the Spirit of Christ, and the Spirit of Glory, reveals and bring praises *and* worship to the Lord Jesus Christ and Almighty God. Let's further examine all of this in a more detailed way and see the functional relationship between the Holy Spirit and the Spirit of Grace, the Spirit of Christ, and the Spirit of Glory.

The Holy Spirit as the Spirit of Grace

When we receive blessings from the Gifts of the Spirit it is due to the Holy Spirit, who is the Spirit of Grace, *functioning as* the Spirit of Grace. The Holy Spirit *reveals* the Spirit of Grace when He pours out God's love, mercy, compassion, and grace *to us* for salvation, or for *whatever other* form the blessings He gives to us may take.[8]

God is love. He not only *has* love, He is love. The love of God is really beyond our ability to fully comprehend because it is so profound and infinite. Even more astounding is the fact that His mercy, compassion, and grace are combined with His love! We can get a glimpse of *God's love* by realizing what He *did*. He sacrificed His own Son,

Jesus, so that we could be partakers of His Divine nature, and have all things that pertain to life and godliness! This is profound love, and pure grace. We can also get a glimpse of *God's grace* by realizing what the Holy Spirit does through the Gifts of the Spirit: He pours out God's love, mercy, compassion and blessings by the Spirit of Grace. This is all done to *bless us, and it is revealed to us by the Holy Spirit functioning as the Spirit of Grace!*[9]

Because of God's infinite love and grace, Jesus went to the cross on our behalf. It was the completed work of the cross by Jesus, which further enabled God to send to us the Holy Spirit and His Gifts! Now, when the Holy Spirit manifests His supernatural Gifts *functioning* as the Spirit of Grace, this further demonstrates God's *continuing grace* to us. **Awesome grace is *provided* for us by God, *secured* for us by Jesus, and continues to be *delivered* to us by the Holy Spirit functioning as the Spirit of Grace. Meditate on this!**

The Holy Spirit as the Spirit of Christ

The Holy Spirit, who is the Spirit of Christ, functions as the Spirit of Christ also. The Spirit of Christ dwells within us by the Holy Spirit. Without the Spirit of Christ we would never get a revelation of the Person of Jesus, His work of the cross, and His present day ministry. Thus, *the Holy Spirit as the Spirit of Christ, testifies of Jesus, just as Jesus said He would do!*[10] God the Father gave the Apostle Peter a revelation that Jesus was the Christ, the Son of the living God. But the revelation *of the significance of the resurrection* of Jesus was not given to Peter until his baptism with the Holy Spirit had occurred on the day of Pentecost. If the revelation which was given to Peter was a blessing *to him*, can you comprehend the blessing *given to us* by having the Spirit of Christ *in us,* revealing the totality of Jesus Christ and His present day ministry *to us?* Let's dig a little further into the details of this gem.

I enjoy ministry dealing with healing. But that is *shallow* unless there is love and understanding of The *One by whose stripes* we are healed: The Lord Jesus Christ. I enjoy ministry dealing with faith. But that too is *shallow* unless there is love and understanding of The *Author* and *Finisher* of our faith: The Lord Jesus Christ. *Nobody* enjoys the Gifts of the Spirit in operation and miracles more than me! Yet, that too is *shallow* unless there is love for the revelation of Jesus who is glorified through the Gifts and the miracles that are performed. We can read and study *about* Jesus from now until "doomsday." But we cannot *know* Him *or truly understand* the significance of His work on the cross, His death, burial, resurrection, or His present day ministry until we receive a revelation of Him by the Spirit of Christ.

The revelation of the Lord Jesus Christ *is always* consistent with the Word of God. When we get a revelation and true understanding *from* the Spirit of Christ of the depth of *grace* God has given *to us* through Jesus Christ, along with a revelation of the *Person, works, and present day ministry of Jesus,* we will have a strong foundation to understand the *function, purpose, and results* of the Gifts as they are manifested by the Holy Spirit. Ask the Holy Spirit to give you a revelation of the fullness of the Lord Jesus Christ.

Jesus allowed Himself to be the sacrifice that was required for us, who through no fault of our own were born into sin, to be reconciled to God through redemption. He was obedient to God by enduring a horrendous death on the cross. This is significant because His death enabled a great exchange to occur and enabled us to be highly acceptable to God.

Because of the death of Jesus on the cross, eternal death *for us* was exchanged for eternal life. Every type of curse known that could afflict us was exchanged for every type of blessing God wants to give to us. Sickness *for us* was exchanged for health. Poverty *for us* was exchanged for prosperity. But best of all, due to the shedding of His blood the sins *of all people* have been remitted. All that is required is to simply accept His sacrifice. Look what *Jesus has done for everybody!* [11]

After being raised from the dead by the Holy Spirit, Christ ascended into Heaven and was *highly* exalted by God. He was seated at the Right Hand of God's majesty. In this position Jesus has a new ministry on your behalf and mine. He performs certain *priestly rituals* before God on our behalf. He *intercedes with prayer* to God on our behalf. And, He acts as *our advocate* before God. This is what Jesus *is doing for us right now.* [12] We may read about it, but it is the Holy Spirit, *functioning as* the Spirit of Christ, *who reveals* the Person, works, and present day ministry of Christ and makes it all *real* to us.

The Holy Spirit enabled the earthly life of Jesus, the Holy Spirit anointed Jesus for a supernatural ministry upon the Earth, the Holy Spirit revealed the glory of God through Jesus, the Holy Spirit enabled Jesus to lay down His life on the cross, and the Holy Spirit enabled Jesus to be raised up from the dead. All of this was done because of God's love and grace *for us*.

Therefore, who *can give us* the revelation, the understanding, the significance, the reality, and the magnificence of the Person, works, and ministry of the Lord Jesus Christ other than the Holy Spirit *functioning as* the Spirit of Christ?

The Holy Spirit as the Spirit of Glory

When the Holy Spirit *functions as* the Spirit of Glory He demonstrates the absolute glorious splendor of God. The Spirit of Glory shows forth the might, power, and sensational miracle working ability of the Holy Spirit to glorify Jesus, *just as Jesus said the Holy Spirit would do!*

We can see from experience that the Spirit of Glory reveals the magnificence, the brilliance, elegance, beauty, and gracefulness of God in a spiritual aura that engenders exaltation and thanksgiving to God. This leads to praise and worship as the presence of Divinity is realized by the people.

Praise gives acknowledgement, recognition, thanksgiving, and honor to God for His greatness, His great works, and for *what great things He has done and is doing.* **Worship** extends love, adoration, devotion, and reverence from *our* heart *to Him for who He is.* As the Spirit of Glory glorifies God, He draws people to glorify God and also draws them to the Lord Jesus Christ. [13]

The Holy Spirit also manifests His Gifts as the Spirit of Glory to honor the Person of Christ, His finished work on the cross, and His present day ministry. [14] Let's get a little deeper insight about this for a moment.

Just hours before going to the cross, Jesus told His disciples that "the hour is come when the Son of Man, meaning Himself, should be glorified." Notice He didn't say crucified. He said glorified. His soul was stirred up, agitated, troubled, so He called out to God saying, "Father, glorify thy Name!" Now check out the response of God to the cry of Jesus, and notice how God responded. The Word says a voice came from Heaven saying, "I have both glorified it, and will glorify it again." God spoke so loudly that the people around Jesus heard Him, and some even thought that it was thunder.

So, we know God speaks by the Holy Spirit. Therefore, this was actually a Word of Knowledge and a Word of Wisdom by the Spirit given directly to Jesus and the people around Him concerning what God *had done*, and *was going to do* again: glorify His Name! The questions then become *how* did God *already* glorify His Name, *how* is He going to glorify it *again*, and *what does this have to do with the Spirit of Glory?*

To begin with, the very conception of Jesus itself was a supernatural event that represented the glory of God as the angels declared. During His earthly life and ministry, Jesus represented and demonstrated the will and work of The Almighty God. This was done in the fullness of God's love, grace, might. By the supernatural manifestation of the Gifts of the Spirit with signs, wonders, and miracles, Jesus demonstrated absolute and t*otal supremacy over all things*; satanic power, the laws of gravity, chemistry and biophysics, death, lack, sickness, diseases, and infirmities of every type. These activities gave glory to God and His Name. [B] This is how God *had* glorified His Name through Jesus *before* Jesus went to the cross.

Now, God is going to glorify His Name through Christ Jesus *again.* Just as the conception, life and ministry of Jesus on earth was supernatural, **His work on the cross, His death, His burial, His defeat of all evil powers and His resurrection, would also be supernatural and therefore glorify the Name of God again!**

As a result of His obedience and accomplishments, God highly exalted Jesus by giving Him a Name above every

---

[B] **The Apostle John said he supposed the world would not be able to hold the books containing the things Jesus did.**

name that is named. Then God caused all of the fullness of the Godhead to dwell in Jesus bodily and made Jesus both Lord and Christ. It is from this standing that Jesus now has a new glorious ministry on behalf of you and me. *The accomplishments of Jesus from the cross to the Throne of God is when God glorified His Name through Jesus, again.*

These accomplishments all represented supernatural acts of God. Any supernatural act of God represents the glory of God. The glory of God is always revealed by the Spirit of Glory when the Gifts of the Spirit are in operation. Therefore, God is still glorifying His Name. This is the connection between the Spirit of Glory, God glorifying His Name, and the Gifts.

Whereas the Spirit of Grace demonstrates the love, mercy, and grace that God has *for us*, and the Spirit of Christ reveals the resurrected Lord Jesus Christ to us, the Spirit of Glory demonstrates the might, power, and miracle-working ability of the Holy Spirit *to glorify* Jesus and God. All miracles glorify Jesus and God, and have the effect of *causing many to believe in Christ Jesus*.[15] Since the Lord Jesus Christ is central to everything pertaining to the Holy Spirit and His Gifts, we can see why the Spirit of Glory glorifies Him so wonderfully when the Gifts are manifested. The Spirit of Grace, the Spirit of Christ, and the Spirit of Glory working together through the Gifts of the Spirit generate beautiful results for both man and God.

Results for Man and God

God the Father, the Lord Jesus Christ, along with the Holy Spirit and His Gifts, all work together in harmony for *our profit and benefit*. The *ultimate result* of the Holy Spirit manifesting His Gifts is to bless man

and bring honor and glory to God. Man is blessed by receiving a revelation of Jesus Christ, receiving salvation and other blessings of various types, and by beholding the glory of God. Glory and honor is brought to God as the people He has created recognize Him, praise Him for His great and mighty works, and worship Him for who He is!

Now let's see an example of how all of this could come together in a practical ministry situation. Suppose through a Gift of the Spirit called the Word of Knowledge, the Holy Spirit identifies a person who is blind in the left eye that He desires to heal. Suppose this person is also an unbeliever. The healing would be a gift due to God's grace secured by Jesus Christ, and manifested by the Holy Spirit as the Spirit of Grace. The Holy Spirit as the Spirit of Christ reveals the presence of Jesus; the One by whose stripes this unbeliever's blindness was healed on the cross. By opening this unbeliever's left blind eye to see, the Holy Spirit now functions as the Spirit of Glory to bring awe, glory, honor, and praise to Jesus.

In this atmosphere of glory and splendor, this unbeliever is overwhelmed by the marvelous gift of sight he has received, praises and worships God with thanksgiving, realizes that Jesus Christ is Lord, and believes on Him for eternal salvation. With Jesus as the *master connection*, here we see the interrelationship and functioning of all of the Godhead with the Gifts of the Holy Spirit. The results are wonderful for man and to God.

God's grace, the grace of the Lord Jesus Christ, the work of the Spirit of Grace, the work of the Spirit of Christ, and the work of the Spirit of Glory are all brought together in harmony by the wonderful Holy Spirit as He manifests

His Gifts. The *Spirit of Grace, the Spirit of Christ, and the Spirit of Glory are interconnected with Jesus when the Gifts are manifested.* We need the *foundation* and *understanding* of this Master Connection to genuinely appreciate the marvelous supernatural Gifts of the precious Holy Spirit. Embrace them! They are marvelous!

Conduct

Since the Gifts of the Spirit confirm the Word of God, we must always endeavor to insure that the Word ministered is correctly divided; meaning correctly analyzed and understood, and is profitable for doctrine, for reproof, for correction, for instruction in righteousness, and is Christ related. [16]

The Almighty God is Holy. The Lord Jesus Christ is Holy. The Holy Spirit is Holy. The Gifts of the Spirit are connected to a Holy God, His Holy Son, and are manifested by His Holy Spirit who is the Spirit of God *and* the Spirit of Christ. Therefore, the Gifts of the Spirit are Holy and separated *from all else* unto God for *His* Divine purposes *only*.

Those through whom the Holy Spirit chooses to operate His Gifts should allow them to flow in a Holy manner. The Gifts of the Spirit should *never* be taken for granted, played with, toyed with, conducted in a cavalier manner, or as some type of exhibition or theatrical performance. To deceitfully handle the Word of God, which the Gifts of the Holy Spirit confirm, or abuse the Gifts of the Spirit could incur the gravest of wrath from Jesus Christ reserved for those He never knew: "depart from me, ye that work iniquity!"[17]

Supporting Scriptures:
The Master Connection
Please read the scriptures

---

[1] Lk 2:25-26, Mt 16:13-17, Eph 1:17-19, Jn 1:1,2, 1 Jn 5:7 Rev 19:11-13
[2] Heb 9:14, 1 Pet 1:11
[3] Jas 1:17
[4] Jn 1:14, 16, 17, Eph 2:8, Rom 5:15, Heb 4:16, 1Pet 5:10, 1Cor 1:4, Zec 12:10, Heb 10:29, 1 Jn 5:7
[5] Eph 3:2, Heb 4:16
[6] Judg 14:5,6,19, 15:15
[7] Is 11:1,2

Spirit of Grace
[8] Heb 10:29
[9] 1 Jn 4:8, Rom 8:32

Spirit of Christ
[10] Rom 8:9, Jn 15:26
[11] Jn 3:16, Rom 5:10, 1Pet 2:24, 2 Cor 8:9, Is 53:5
[12] Phil 2:9, Heb 2:17, 3:1, 7:22-25, 1 Jn 2:1, Heb 8:6

Spirit of Glory
[13] Jn 16:13,14,
[14] Jn 12:28, 17:1, 1 Pet 1:18-21, Heb 2:9
[15] Jn 2:11, Mk 2:12, Lk 5:26, Jn 7:31
[16] Mk16:20, 2Ti 2:15, 3Ti 3:16
[17] 2 Cor4:2, Mt 7:20-23

CHAPTER FOUR

THE SUPERNATURAL GIFTS OF THE HOLY SPIRIT

The spectacular supernatural Gifts of the Holy Spirit are exclusive gifts given freely to us from God. These are *spiritual* Gifts of infinite power and ability, knowledge and wisdom, and communication *from* God that are available to operate *through you.*

All nine of these Gifts are Divine supernatural and extraordinary endowments that are performed *only* by the Holy Spirit, and each Gift can be *identified* one from another by *specific* criteria. These types of Gifts are different from other gifts God has set in the church such as gifts of government, teaching, exhortation, and so forth. God gives the Gifts of the Spirit along with pastors and other Five Fold Ministry Gifts to build His church. Yet many do not operate in *any* of *the supernatural* Gifts of the Holy Spirit or even work with others that do! The spiritual Gifts of the Holy Spirit are supernatural acts of God's mighty power and superb greatness. They are for His church, and we need them!

The Holy Spirit and His Gifts are *absolutely sovereign.* It has been my experience to find that the Holy Spirit can manifest His Gifts *through us*, as He wills, or, He can manifest His Gifts *independently of us*, as He wills. Non believers as well as Believers can receive blessings from the manifestation of His Gifts. This may surprise some, but the manifestations of His Gifts can even be independent of faith exercised by the person through whom the Holy Spirit is operating. Likewise, the manifestations of His Gifts can operate independently of the faith of the person the Holy Spirit chooses to bless.

With *one exception*, in over twenty-five years of ministering by the Gifts of the Holy Spirit, I have *never* seen a manifestation that wasn't specific and accurate, or that failed to produce the blessing for the condition or person for whom it was revealed. *Never!* That one exception occurred when a person with a particular condition revealed by the Holy Spirit *did not want to be healed* because, as she later expressed, she felt that her condition was an asset "to her ministry." Astounding, but true!

Now back to faith. From my experience, I can assure you that *none* of the *results* from the manifestations of the Gifts relied upon *my personal faith*. It seems to me that *obedience* to reveal, or do what the Holy Spirit instructs, is my only role. Everything else is up to *Him*. I simply believe that He is God and that with God, nothing is impossible. This is altogether different from exercising your own *personal faith* to receive something from God.

To me, this proves the absolute and total sovereignty of the Holy Spirit to manifest His Gifts as *He wills* and through whomever He chooses. *We* cannot cause any of the Gifts of the Spirit to be manifested through us or through anyone else, at *our own will*. Nobody "has a Gift" of the Holy Spirit. Only the Holy Spirit has the Gifts, and they are under *His* control and will. Likewise, nobody can bestow any Gift of the Holy Spirit *upon another*. That is the sovereign right of the Holy Spirit *only*.

Even though scripture proves that the Gifts of the Spirit were in operation in the Old Testament, the earthly life and ministry of Jesus Christ, and in the Early Church, there are many Believers today who have little knowledge and understanding of the Gifts and how they operate. There are some who feel there is *no need for them*. If it was desirable that people in the Early Church not be ignorant of *spiritual* gifts which were in need *then*, we certainly should not be ignorant of them today because during the perilous times in which *we are living*, our need for them is great.[1] Having the marvelous Gifts of the Spirit operate through you to help others is one of the most exhilarating blessings you will ever experience. And it can happen with *you*. Let's now find out what the Gifts do and how they are administered.

The Gifts and their Administration

There are nine spiritual Gifts of the Holy Spirit. They are ***The Word of Wisdom, The Word of Knowledge, The Discerning of spirits, The Working of Miracles, The Gifts of Healings, The Gift of Faith, The Gift of Tongues, The Interpretation of Tongues, and The Gift of Prophecy***.[2]

These Gifts appear to fall into three different groups, or categories, which express God's Divine knowledge, God's Divine power and ability, and God's method of Divine communication. Therefore we have: **The Gifts of Divine Revelation Knowledge**. These Gifts supernaturally give to us insight and disclose something to us that God knows. **The Gifts of Divine Power and Ability**. These Gifts demonstrate supernatural power, ability, and works of God. **The Gifts of Divine Vocal Communication**. These Gifts give supernatural information from God to us in languages known and unknown.

The Gifts in each group have a similar function but each Gift is different *in the manner of its operation*. The three groups *are different from one another* and also have different functions. Let me give you a natural example of the functional principle I'm talking about.

If we look at the subject of transportation, we find that there are *three modes* of transportation that exist. There's transportation by land, by air, and by sea. Each mode is different than the other two and each mode has its own distinguishing features and methods. Therefore, on land we can travel by foot, bus, or roller skates. By air we can travel by plane, balloon, or rocket. On sea we can travel by boat, submarine, or by swimming. But *all* modes have one central characteristic in common: transportation. This same principle applies *to each* of the three groups that make up the nine Gifts of the Holy Spirit.

Divine Harmony in Administration

Now that we understand what the Gifts are, do, and the functional categories they fit into, let me make a few comments that I hope will help all of us to understand how the Holy Spirit *administers* His Gifts through us *in harmony with* the Lord Jesus Christ and Almighty God.

There are different and diverse kinds of Gifts, but they are all administered through us by the same Holy Spirit.[3] He is the source and originator of them all. There are distinctive types of ministries, but it is the same Lord Jesus Christ who is served.[4] In other words, the ministry of the deacon is different than the ministry of the apostle, the ministry of the pastor is different than the ministry of the worship leader, the ministry of a prayer warrior is different than someone in the ministry of helps. But *they all* serve the same Lord Jesus Christ with the Gifts. There are distinctive, effective, and various types of mighty works, but it is the same God who shows forth His mighty power *through those works* and who inspires *us*, empowers *us*, and works through all of *us* with the Gifts [5] All of these achievements and abilities are brought together and administered by the Holy Spirit.

The Gifts are for good and profit. The Holy Spirit allocates several Gifts to individual persons in the Body of Christ as *He wills*. The Holy Spirit, the Lord Jesus Christ, and God the Father all work together for the same purpose and outcome; for They are One.[6] But as we have discovered, the center and essence of all things pertaining to the Holy Spirit and His Gifts is the Lord Jesus Christ. [A]

The example given by scripture to illustrate this principle of *harmonious administration* is the functioning of the human body.[7] Each individual part is different, yet all are essential and must work together. The brain needs the heart. The tongue needs the ears. The fingers need the hand.

God wants diversity and harmony among the people through whom the Gifts operate, just as there is diversity and harmony between the Holy Spirit and His Gifts, the Lord Jesus Christ, and God Himself. No person, no group, no church or denomination has a monopoly on the Gifts of the Spirit. *The Gifts are for us all who belong to Jesus Christ!* But we should be in harmony with God and with each other. The agent for this harmony is love!

The Sovereignty of the Holy Spirit

As a sovereign member of the Godhead, the Holy Spirit is not limited to *anything*. He works with Jesus and the Father but He has total authority to independently manifest His Gifts *whenever* He wants to, *wherever* He

[A] See the Master Connection Page 27

wants to, and *through whomever* He wants to. This means He can operate *through you*, at anytime, and in any place for His own purpose. Some people think that signs, wonders, and miracles portrayed by the Gifts are only done by God *to confirm* the Word. The Holy Spirit does use the Gifts to confirm the Word of God, but He *does not limit* them to this role. They are also used *to bring blessings* to people anytime, anywhere. Let's get a glimpse of what I'm talking about from scripture. We'll look at the ministry of Jesus since His ministry is always the best example.

From the Book of Luke we find that many people came and pressed upon Jesus to hear the Word of God. Because there was a steady force of people pressing up against Him, He needed some room! He was standing by a lake and saw two ships where fisherman had gone out of them and were washing their nets. Therefore, they had finished fishing and were cleaning up their nets. In fact, they had been fishing all night and had caught nothing.

So Jesus went aboard the ship belonging to Simon Peter and asked him to thrust out into the water a little further. This way He could be further back from the crowd. Jesus then taught the Word of God to the people from *out of the ship!*

Now watch this. After He had finished speaking, Jesus told Simon to launch out into the deep and let down the nets for a haul of fish. Jesus knew where the fish were through a Word of Knowledge. Simon obeyed and caught so many fish that the nets began to break and he had to call upon his partners to come and help fill up two ships. **This is a classic example of the Holy Spirit confirming the Word of God with signs, wonders, and miracles through the Gifts of the Spirit, *after* the Word is taught or preached.**[8]

Yet on other occasions the Gifts *were not* used to

confirm the Word of God, but used just to be a blessing to people. The Working of Miracles to turn water into wine because the wine had run out at a wedding, and the Word of Knowledge telling the disciples where to go to find money to pay taxes, are just a few examples of the Gifts of the Spirit operating through Jesus to simply be a blessing to people by meeting their needs.

Now you may be thinking "Sure, but *that* was Jesus". True! But let's look at Stephen. Stephen wasn't Jesus, he wasn't even an apostle. He was chosen by the apostles to do *the work of a deacon!* But, he was a man full of faith and power who did great wonders and miracles among the people. He was full of the Holy Ghost, which accounts for his power, and did great wonders and miracles; which means that the Gifts of the Holy Spirit operated through him, too. Why not through you?[9]

The Holy Spirit is sovereign and He has no limitations as to when, where, how, or through whom He selects to manifest His Gifts to confirm the Word of God, or to simply bless people. You too can be used anytime at any place *if* it is your desire, *and His will!* But always remember, the spiritual Gifts of the Holy Spirit are never manifested through us because of *our* ability, holiness, or power. They are manifested *only* because of God's ability, power, and righteousness. And He does this to glorify His Son Jesus Christ, to demonstrate the Kingdom of God, and to bless people with His infinite love, mercy, and grace. [10]

Supporting Scriptures:
The Supernatural Gifts of the Holy Spirit
Please read the scriptures

---

[1] 1Cor 12:1, 2 Ti 3:1-5, 1 Ti 4:1, 2, 2 Ti 4:3,4.

[2] 1 Cor 12:7-11
[3] 1 Cor 12:4
[4] 1 Cor 12:5
[5] 1 Cor 12:6
[6] 1 Jn 5:7
[7] 1 Cor 12:7
[8] Luke 5:1-7
[9] Acts 6:2-8
[10] Acts 3:11,12

THE GIFTS OF DIVINE REVELATION KNOWLEDGE

As you may remember, the Word of Wisdom, the Word of Knowledge, and the Discerning of spirits, are in the group of supernatural Gifts that we call the Gifts of Divine Revelation Knowledge. These Gifts express, reveal, show, give insight, or disclose something to us that is known by God. These Gifts *themselves*, whether singularly or collectively, are not all knowing; but *their source is*. Their source is God. God has a mind, and He is all knowing about all people, places, things, conditions, and events past, present, and future. These Gifts of the Holy Spirit often overlap in their use and in the manner in which they are experienced. They sometimes dovetail and coordinate with Gifts of the Spirit which are in *other* groups. *God can elect to use these Gifts* to disclose to us the things He knows. These are wonderful and marvelous Gifts. We will begin with the Word of Wisdom.

Chapter Five

THE WORD OF WISDOM

The Word of Wisdom is a supernatural revelation from God of His knowledge concerning a *future* person, place, thing, condition, or event. Those are the specific criteria that identify this Gift.

When we do a detailed study of the word "wisdom," as it is associated with this Gift, we find that it means wise. And in this context the word "wise" is connected to knowledge. In addition, one of the characteristics of *this kind* of knowledge pertains *to the future*. God has the ability to penetrate the future regarding the knowledge of all things. He can then reveal to us, through the Word of Wisdom, whatever extent of His foresight and knowledge that He desires to disclose.[1]

The Word of Wisdom can be given by the Holy Spirit through an inward voice heard only by the person intended to receive it. It can be given in a vision, a dream, or through prophecy. There are times when part of the revelation is received, and there are times when the full revelation is received. There are times when the revelation can be fully understood, and there are times when the revelation is not fully understood until after what was partially revealed is completely fulfilled.[A]

The Gift of the Word of Wisdom given by the Holy

[A] See the Florida Assignment Page 195.

Spirit is different from *natural* wisdom. Natural wisdom is available to *all*. That's why the Word of God says, "If *any* man lacks wisdom let him ask God who gives *to all* men liberally." [2] But the Gift of The Word of Wisdom given by the Holy Spirit *is not* given *to all*. It is given *only* to those whom the Holy Spirit selects according to His own will.

In the Old Testament

In the Old Testament, the Word of Wisdom was used in various settings and for various purposes. For example, the great prophet Isaiah received a Word of Wisdom from the Lord to give a message to a king named Hezekiah. The message given in the Word of Wisdom was that days were going *to come*, when all that was in the king's house, including all of his treasure and the things he had inherited, would be carried off into Babylon and that nothing would be left. The message even told what was going to happen to the king's sons.[3] We know this was a Word of Wisdom because it came from the Lord to the prophet regarding what *was going* to happen to the king, *in the future*.

Noah was a man who walked closely with God. He warned Noah that He *was going to destroy* the Earth with water because of violence and corruption on the Earth. He then instructed Noah as to how to build an ark so that he and his household could be saved.[4] We know that this was a Word of Wisdom because the event came to pass, *in the future*, just as it was revealed to Noah.

In The Life and Ministry of Jesus Christ

In the earthly life and ministry of the Lord Jesus Christ, we see some marvelous examples of the Word of

Wisdom in operation. Look at this!

Jesus was in the process of leaving the Temple when His disciples came to Him and brought to His attention all of the beautiful surrounding buildings associated with the Temple. Then a Word of Wisdom came forth through the Holy Spirit to Jesus and He told His disciples that all of the things they saw related to the Temple and its surrounding buildings *would be* torn down. He further told them the extent of the devastation by saying that there wouldn't be one stone left upon another that wouldn't be torn down.[5] We know this was a Word of Wisdom because *later*, soldiers in the Roman army destroyed the Temple and its surrounding buildings just as Jesus had said, and the results were just as He had said they would be.

Next, we see another superb example of the Word of Wisdom operating through Jesus. On the first day of a feast called "the feast of unleavened bread," Jesus told His disciples to go and prepare for the Passover where they would eat. The disciples didn't know where to go! Jesus told them to go into the city and a man would meet them with a pitcher of water. This is a Word of Wisdom describing a *future* event of something that was going to occur. Then, they were to follow the man into the house where he entered, and ask the Master of the house where was the guest chamber where Jesus and His disciples could eat. Jesus told Peter and John that the Master of the house would show them a large, furnished, upper room.[6] This is the Word of Knowledge at work because the furnished room was a fact *existing at that time*, known to God, which He revealed to Jesus by the Holy Spirit. This is an example as to how the Gifts can overlap. The Word of Knowledge was working in combination with the Word of Wisdom since Jesus was speaking to Peter and John about *what existed*, and what they would also find *in the future* as they went forth. Wow!

Here we see the Word of Wisdom operating through Jesus in remarkable detail. The man Jesus spoke about was not carrying a pitcher of water at the time Jesus was speaking. This was going to occur in the *future*. The events Jesus spoke of came to pass exactly as He described them. Again, this is a perfect example of the Word of Wisdom and the Word of Knowledge working together. We shall discuss the Word of Knowledge a little later.

Another, even more spectacular experience occurred in the life and ministry of Jesus when multiple Gifts of the Spirit came into operation along with the Word of Wisdom. Jesus was informed that a friend named Lazarus was sick and had died. He told His disciples that the death of Lazarus was so that the glory of God could be manifested. Knowing that the glory of God, pertaining to this situation, was to be manifested *in the future* makes this a Word of Wisdom that Jesus had received.

After four days, Jesus came to the tomb of Lazarus. The Gift of Faith dropped down so deeply into the spirit of Jesus that He commanded Lazarus, by name, to come forth out of the tomb. Then, the Working of Miracles went into operation as the Holy Spirit raised Lazarus from the dead. The glory of God was shown forth just as Jesus had received it from a Word of Wisdom, and had told His disciples four days earlier.[7] A little later on we're going to see an experience that occurred with me that in *some ways* was a *little bit* similar, and very awesome![B] The Word of Wisdom is a marvelous Gift of the Spirit and it is still in operation today. Desire the Holy Spirit to use this Gift *through you*.

[B] See the Florida Assignment Pg.195

In the Early Church

Now we're going to see a good example of the Word of Wisdom in operation during the Early Church era.

On his way to Jerusalem, the Apostle Paul stayed several days at the house of an evangelist named Philip. A prophet named Agabus came by to visit Paul with a message from God. Agabus went over to Paul, took Paul's belt and tied *his own* feet and hands with Paul's belt. Then he said, "Thus saith the Holy Ghost: so shall the Jews that are at Jerusalem bind the man that owneth this girdle and shall deliver him into the hands of the Gentiles."[8] We know this is a Word of Wisdom because the prophet is revealing something that was going to happen to Paul at Jerusalem *in the future.*

There's another fact that may be significant here. God could have sent this information directly to Paul by the Holy Spirit. However, by choosing to send the message by a prophet seems to indicate that God not only wanted Paul to know the message was from Him, but for Paul to also believe it without doubt. You see, Paul being a Jew was very aware of the creditability of those standing in the Office of the Prophet. In the Old Testament, if someone claimed to be a prophet of God spoke a word in the Lord's Name which the Lord did not tell him to speak, or spoke in the name of other gods, or said, "Thus saith the Lord, or thus saith the Spirit of God," then gave a message and the message wasn't true or didn't come to pass, that "prophet" would be considered a "false prophet" and could be put to death. Paul would have known this, and therefore he most likely would have paid close attention to what this New Testament prophet had to say, and believe him.[9]

God can speak words through an angel, He can speak

through another person, or He can speak directly through the Holy Spirit. In this case, the Word of Wisdom was clearly a warning from God, spoken through a prophet, telling what was going to happen to Paul at Jerusalem in the *future*. Finally, let's look at several experiences from my own life and ministry related to the Word of Wisdom. We will see how relevant and valuable this Gift is for us today.

In the Life and Ministry of the Author

During a period of prolonged prayer in preparation for services at a church in California, the Holy Spirit gave me a Word of Wisdom in a vision. The vision showed an execution table covered with a white sheet and large, strong, restraining belts to strap the prisoner down for lethal injection. I knew someone was scheduled to be executed. This was a Word of Wisdom because it pertained to an event that *was going to occur in the future*.

While ministering at the actual church service, the Holy Spirit caused me to know that this vision had connection to someone in the congregation and that I should reveal it. After it was revealed, a woman known to be a devout Believer came forth and told the rest of the story. It happened that a distraught woman whose son was scheduled to be executed by lethal injection had called this Believer out of desperation. The Believer indicated that she didn't quite know how to handle a situation like this. Immediately the Holy Spirit prompted me as to what should be done and I informed the congregation accordingly.

The congregation was instructed to pray for mercy and to pray that the Lord would touch the Governor's heart to either issue a pardon or commute the death sentence to life in prison. The church was also instructed to send an envoy to the son to insure his salvation through Christ Jesus and inform him of what happened in the church service so he would know that God knew all about his situation. The devout Believer was instructed to visit the mother of the prisoner and pray with her for peace, and to give her comfort by letting her know that God knew all about the situation because it was revealed by a visiting minister at the church. Thank God for the Word of Wisdom because, as you can see, it is very practical and much needed today.

Now let's look at a very interesting situation where the Word of Wisdom and the Word of Knowledge complimented one another. While ministering with the Gifts of the Spirit at another California church, the Holy Spirit revealed to me that there was a young man in the congregation carrying a knife, and gave a detailed description of the knife. It had a sharp, shiny, mirror-like silver blade about four inches long and a beautiful pearl handle. This was a Word of Knowledge in action. Then the young man was instructed to come forth for prayer and to surrender the knife to the pastor, or else, *some day* he would commit a serious crime with *that* knife. That was instruction given by the Holy Spirit, and a Word of Wisdom revealing what would happen *in the future* if he was disobedient. A young man came forth for prayer but *would not* surrender the knife. That event occurred about twenty years ago.

Now get this! While talking with that same church pastor several months ago his wife intervened and said, "Eugene, do you remember that young man you prayed for in the church that had the pearl-handled knife but wouldn't turn it in?" I didn't remember until she gave me the details! "Well," she continued, "He was arrested several months ago and is now in jail for killing somebody with *that* knife." That was the tragic conclusion of not totally heeding instructions that were given with a Word of Wisdom twenty years ago. We need the Word of Wisdom today, and we need to obey the Spirit of God when He gives us instructions.

Another blessing resulting from a Word of Wisdom is included here because it is one of the latest manifestations of the Gifts of the Spirit given to me that had *personal* implications. One day around mid morning, our youngest son, his wife, his two year old daughter and two month old son, came to visit and to spend the day with my wife and me. My son came to oversee a new computer and telephone installation that was scheduled to be done. While awaiting the arrival of the company's installation technician, I had a *desire* to pray.

After about ten minutes of lying down in a private area and *quietly* praying in the Spirit, a Word of Wisdom manifested to me in a vision. In the vision it was night time and it was as though I was seeing *through the eyes of someone else* driving a vehicle. This driver was approaching the rear end of a dark or black SUV-type vehicle which seemed to be slowing down. Unless the trailing vehicle could be stopped, rear end contact with the vehicle in front appeared imminent.

Since the installer was late in arriving, my daughter-in-law drove my wife and the children to a store for refreshments. But before leaving I pulled her aside and told her to drive with great wisdom, and be sure to drive a good distance behind any car in front of her, especially if it was a black SUV-type vehicle. She agreed, and they left and returned without incident.

My son and his family left to return home about 10:00 P.M., carrying my wife as an extra passenger to visit our daughter. They were admonished to drive with great wisdom and reminded that some Friday night drivers are often reckless. Remembering the Word of Wisdom received earlier, I also prayed for their safety. Around 12:00 midnight, my son called to tell me that they all had arrived safely but that an "incident" nearly occurred during the trip. Here's what happened.

My son was driving in the right lane when another vehicle entered onto the highway at a high rate of speed and failed to yield to on going traffic. My son was alert and swerved to the left to avoid collision but had to instantly brake to avoid running into the back of a black SUV-type vehicle directly in front of him that was going very slowly! This was exactly what the Holy Spirit had shown to me in the vision earlier during the day while I was praying.

What would the Holy Spirit have us to learn from this incident? He wants us to know that He is here to help us and warn us of impending trouble that can be stopped through prayer. When urged to pray, pray! This is often when the Holy Spirit will tell us or show us things *to come, just as Jesus said He would do!* The Holy Spirit does this through the Word of Wisdom. Now we see how valuable the Word of Wisdom is for us today. And remember, it can be available *for you too!*

Supporting Scriptures:
The Word of Wisdom
Please read the scriptures

---

[1] Acts 2:23
[2] Jas 1:5
[3] 2 Ki 20:16-18
[4] Gen 6:12-18

[5] Mk 13:1,2
[6] Mk 14:12-16
[7] Jn 11:1-6, 40, 43, 44
[8] Acts 21:8-11
[9] Deut 18:20, 13:1-5

Chapter Six

THE WORD OF KNOWLEDGE

God is *omniscient.* This means He is *all knowing,* informed, and has infinite *understanding* of all things. He has full, crystal clear, thorough, and complete knowledge and understanding of everything that is past, present, and future. This knowledge and understanding pertains to all realms, whether it's *this sense realm* where we perceive things through our natural senses, *or other spirit realms.* It is through the Gifts of the Spirit, along with the Word of God, that He discloses *to us* the things that He knows.

The Word of Knowledge is a supernatural manifestation by the Holy Spirit to reveal certain facts known to God that pertain to something *which has occurred in the past* or something *that is occurring at the present time.* Those specific criteria identify this Gift. The Word of Knowledge has absolutely nothing to do with common or intellectual human knowledge. It has nothing to do with being smart, or having many scholastic degrees, a high IQ, or having great knowledge of the Bible. No, this Gift is a Divine *supernatural* manifestation given by the Holy Spirit to flow through those of His choosing. It is used by the Holy Spirit to give directions, reveal danger, sickness, pain, physical disorder, or *anything* which *is occurring at the present, or has occurred in the past* that God knows and wants to reveal. Let's look at a few examples of the Word of Knowledge from the Old Testament, the earthly life and ministry of Jesus Christ, the Early Church, and from my own life and ministry.

In the Old Testament

The Lord told Moses to go to Pharaoh and tell Pharaoh, "The Lord says let my people go that they may hold a feast unto me in the wilderness." Then the Lord told Aaron, the brother of Moses, to go into the wilderness to meet Moses.[1] Here we see two things shown by the Word of Knowledge. First, the Lord knew exactly where Moses was *at that present time*. Secondly, the Lord was directing Aaron *where* to go and *what* to do: go into the wilderness, and meet with Moses.

When the Lord told Moses to make a Tabernacle where He could be worshipped, men of great talent were needed to help Moses get the job done. So through a Word of Knowledge, God told Moses who He was sending to help get the job done, then gave to Moses the man's qualifications![2] The Lord called a man named Bazaleel whom He had filled with the Spirit of God in wisdom, understanding, in knowledge and in *all* manner of workmanship. In addition, the Lord revealed to Moses that He had given helpers to Bazaleel to make all things according to the commandment given by God to Moses for making the Tabernacle. Here we see *current facts* known to God and revealed to Moses by the Holy Spirit through a Word of Knowledge. It related to the person, and his qualifications, that God had prepared to help Moses build the Tabernacle according to God's pattern. Now, let's move on to see the Word of Knowledge in operation through the life and ministry of Jesus.

In the Life and Ministry of Jesus Christ

In the earthly life and ministry of Jesus Christ, we see fantastic examples of the Word of Knowledge in action. After Jesus performed the miracle creating enough food to feed five thousand people from five loaves of bread and two fish, He compelled His disciples to cross over the Sea of Galilee to the other side *from* where they and great multitudes of people had been gathered. While the disciples were gone, Jesus went up into a mountain to pray. When evening had come, the disciples were far out on the sea. Jesus was alone, far from them, on the land. Scripture tells us that later on *at night*, Jesus *saw them* toiling and struggling because the wind was against them. So He went to them walking on the water so fast that He could have passed them by.[3]

Now, how in the world could Jesus, looking with natural eyesight, see someone *that far* out in the water when it was *at night?* He couldn't! Nobody could. But remember, He was in prayer. What had to happen was that while praying, the Lord gave Him a vision. It had to be a Word of Knowledge given through the vision that enabled Jesus to see His disciples on the sea and the problems they were having, even though He was on land at night! The Word of Knowledge given pertained to events that were happening at that particular time. So He went to save them. Very often the Word of Knowledge is given by the Holy Spirit in visions, especially while praying, and through dreams.[4]

Another great example of the Word of Knowledge operating through Jesus occurred when He was tired and thirsty. He asked a woman He had encountered at a well to give Him a drink of water from the well. After having a discussion about drinking the water from the well and drinking the special kind of water He had to offer, Jesus asked her to call her husband. She told Him she had no husband. After confirming to her that He knew that, Jesus told her that she had had five husbands and that the man she was currently living with *was not* her husband.[5] Busted! But notice this, Jesus didn't put her down. She knew in her heart that the condition she was living in wasn't good, so why rub it in? Jesus knew that the love of God could change her condition from the inside out. He never put people down. In fact, she ran back into the city and told the people about the great prophet she had met. But how did Jesus *know* that she had five husbands in the *past* and was *presently* living with another man? The Holy Spirit revealed it to Him through a Word of Knowledge.

On another occasion, we see the Word of Knowledge in operation through Jesus regarding taxes. An issue arose as to whether Jesus should pay Temple taxes to the government. Jesus made the decision that taxes should be paid for both Him and His disciples. However they didn't have the money. Through a Word of Knowledge, Jesus told Peter to go into the sea, look into the mouth of the first fish he caught, and he would find money to pay the taxes.[6] In those days money existed in the form of small coins that easily could fit in the mouth of a large fish.

This is the Word of Knowledge in operation because Jesus knew where *the money* was *at that particular time*. All the disciples had to do was to get the fish and take the money to pay the taxes. Jesus hasn't changed, neither has the Holy Spirit, nor the Word of Knowledge. Next, let's look at the Word of Knowledge in operation in the Early Church.

In the Early Church

In the Early Church period, the Apostle Peter went upon a house top to pray. Remember, although there are exceptions, the manifestation of the Gifts of Divine Revelation Knowledge frequently occurs during times of prayer. Peter fell into a trance and had a vision that was somewhat disturbing to him. He was thinking about the vision when the Spirit of God spoke to him and told him that three men were looking for him. Then the Spirit of God directed him to get up, go down, and go with the men doubting nothing because He, the Holy Spirit, had sent them.

Here we see important information and directions given to Peter through a Word of Knowledge with authenticity verified by the Holy Spirit Himself. This Word of Knowledge pertained to the *present*: Three men seek you. It *gave directions*: get up, go down, and go with them doubting nothing. It also *gave assurance and comfort*: I, the Holy Spirit sent them to you. Peter obeyed the instructions given to him by the Holy Spirit and the results were that a Roman Centurion and his whole household were saved.[7] This is so awesome!

In the Life and Ministry of the Author

Now let's see some examples of the Word of Knowledge operating in my life and ministry. My parents were *staunch* Baptist Believers who didn't know *anything* about the Gifts of the Spirit. My mother however, was somewhat open to my teachings on the subject.

Shortly after my father had gone home to be with the Lord, I drove my mother down to the motor vehicle agency to get my father's car registered again. Apparently, the Holy Spirit thought this was an excellent time for my mother to be further educated about the Gifts of the Spirit in normal settings because, while in line sitting in the car, He brought to my attention a man leaning up against a wall and told me that the man was a fugitive running from the Law. I turned to my mother and said, "See that man over there up against the wall? He's a criminal and the police are looking for him!" She looked at me as though to say, "Are you for real, or what!" Minutes later police came seemingly from everywhere, threw the man around, put handcuffs on him, and drove him away in a police car.

This was a Word of Knowledge given to me by the Holy Spirit, just like a Word of Knowledge was given to Jesus about the woman in Samaria who had had five husbands, and was living with a man that wasn't her husband.

Here's what's interesting to notice. The only information the Holy Spirit gave to me through this Word of Knowledge was that the man was a criminal, and that the police were looking for him. This was a Word of Knowledge because it dealt *only* with the man's *present* status. The Holy Spirit *did not* reveal if the man would be caught, or *when* in the future the man would be caught. If He had, that would have been a Word of Wisdom because the information would have dealt with events that *were to occur in the future*. This was a Word of Knowledge given about a man, that the police action simply confirmed.

Remember now, my mother was raised in a Baptist church like me and didn't know too much about the Gifts of the Spirit. She turned to me and said, "My mother said to stay away from people like you!" To this very day I break out in laughter when I remember what she said to me, and *how* she said it. But the incident provided me an excellent opportunity to talk more about the Gifts of the Spirit, and especially the Word of Knowledge which we had just experienced. She learned a lot more about the Holy Spirit, and now she too has gone home to be with the Lord. But notice! I wasn't in a pulpit when this happened. Listen, the

Holy Spirit can manifest His Gifts through anyone, at any time, and in any place He wills. This includes through *you*. Desire to be used by Him!

Years ago my wife and I were ministering at a church in Northern California when the Holy Spirit through a Word of Knowledge revealed that there was a deaf person in the congregation that He wanted to heal. A lady came forth and to my surprise was holding a little baby about eight or nine months old. Clapping loudly on the baby's right and left side of the ears brought no response. The baby was indeed deaf. The mother then informed us that the baby was scheduled for surgery the next day in hopes of restoring *some* hearing. I then looked over to my wife and said, "Pray and ask the Lord to tell us the name of the doctor who is going to perform this baby's surgery." I had never asked her anything like *that* before. My wife looked at me as though to say, "Are you kidding me?" But then she began to quietly pray "in the Spirit." And so did I.

After a minute or so, my wife gave me a name the Holy Spirit had revealed to her. It was the *exact same* name I too had received from the Spirit. This was a specific Word of Knowledge from the Holy Spirit giving each of us, independently, the exact same information. Turning to the child's mother I asked her who was, "Dr. So and So," and spoke out the name given to us by the Holy Spirit. The mother lost all control and yelled out, "He's the doctor that's going to operate on my baby tomorrow!"

We assured the mother that the Holy Spirit didn't reveal all of this information in vain and that the Lord Jesus Christ was the greatest of all healers. After praying in a *very specific way*, the Lord opened the baby's ears to hear. The baby's head turned to the direction of the noise made by the clapping of hands near the ears on both the left and right side. Praise God!

On another occasion, several churches had sponsored us to hold public evangelistic meetings in Dover, Delaware. During one of the services, the Holy Spirit revealed to my wife through a Word of Knowledge that someone was concerned and worried about a *straw* roof. Wait a minute. Picture this. We're in America! Someone *in America* is concerned about a *straw* roof? This is where the rubber meets the road because if we told that to the several thousand people who were in attendance and nobody responded, they would really wonder about us. But we knew that the Holy Spirit is *always* right, so we revealed this information to the people.

After a long minute or so, a lady sitting far in the back of the auditorium came forth. She stated that a storm had destroyed the roof of her family home, that it had to be replaced, and that she needed to see about it. The lady was African. She had been praying because of her concern about the straw roof of her home *in Africa!* The Word of Knowledge through my wife confirmed to this lady that the Lord had heard her prayers. Whoa! Can you believe the comfort and assurance she must have received knowing that *the Lord knew* what was going on, and was working on her behalf? The Lord knows everything about our concerns in detail; and distance is no barrier to Him. Trust Him!

A similar manifestation occurred recently as I was ministering at a men's outdoor service in Southern California. The Holy Spirit revealed to me a person attending, and, a beautiful *black* Harley Davidson-looking motorcycle. I knew that there was some kind of connection between the two that also pertained to the state of North Dakota. A man in his early fifties wearing blue jeans responded to the revelation. He indicated that he wanted a "*black* Harley," and to go back home to start a motorcycle ministry. I asked him where was "back home." He said, "North Dakota!" God put His ministry plan into this man's heart, and then confirmed it to him through a Word of Knowledge from someone else. Fantastic!

While in practice, a patient that I had never known or seen before came to the office for care. She was totally overwhelmed by fear. We considered the possibility that she may require oral sedation or possibly even intravenous sedation to calm her down for treatment. Now you'll see how practical and beneficial the Word of Knowledge can be.

While trying to arrest her fear, the Holy Spirit through a Word of Knowledge suddenly gave me two valuable pieces of information about her *at that time* which changed everything. "You go to a Baptist church, don't you?" I asked. She looked at me with disbelief. "You also sing in the Choir, don't you?" I said. "How did you know *that*?" she responded. I told her it was the Holy Spirit who had just supernaturally informed me, and that furthermore her steps were ordered of the Lord. I assured her that He wouldn't send her to me unless I was going to take excellent care of her and not hurt her. I told her she wasn't given a spirit of fear, but of power, love, a sound mind, and that I wasn't about to displease Jesus by hurting her! With watery eyes she smiled, relaxed, received treatment, and became one of our finest referral sources.

But notice this. The Holy Spirit knew this woman's disposition! He also knew the doctor He wanted her to see. He didn't manifest a Word of Knowledge to me as a minister. This wasn't in church. I wasn't in a pulpit. I was simply doing my job. Your job may be different than mine and your services may be different. But regardless of the situation you may find yourself in, the Holy Spirit desires to *use you* to glorify Jesus and bless *others* just as He *used me* to calm and help that patient. Be open to Him.

It is always interesting to see the lengths to which some people will go when their situation is desperate and they know that only God can help them. The next case I'm going to share with you is quite a testimony to the Word of Knowledge *and faith*. Here is the background.

The Lord gave me great favor with a highly respected and well known medical doctor in New York City's Chinatown. Through him the Lord opened the doors for me to minister in several large house churches where the congregations ranged anywhere from forty to eighty people, jam packed. Because of the multiple dialects spoken there were always two or three people translating the message. But in addition to ministering in the house churches, this doctor would open up the huge waiting room in his private practice office and ask me to minister to his patients and others from the community. Although I knew nothing about his patients' medical conditions, the Holy Spirit would reveal their problems which the doctor would confirm, and then verify their healing. This was usually done on Friday and Saturday afternoons. One Friday, a very remarkable event occurred. Here's what happened.

A Word of Knowledge revealed that there was a person with very severe and terrible itching that the Lord wanted to heal. Nobody responded! I simply placed the problem into the hands of the Lord and continued ministering. Now let's fast forward to the upcoming Sunday service at one of the large House churches, and we'll see why nobody responded that past Friday.

During the testimony portion of the Sunday morning service, an elderly woman came forth and gave her testimony. Her daughter and a small baby were present with her.

Although she herself spoke in Chinese, her remarks were translated by two other people in different Chinese dialects. When she finished speaking there was a tremendous outburst of clapping hands and praising God. The doctor then leaned over to me and explained what the commotion was all about. From her testimony this is what happened.

On the previous Friday afternoon, this grandmother was in the doctor's office and saw the miracles which were occurring. She immediately called her daughter who lived in San Francisco, California and said, "Quick, quick, bring the baby, there are miracles going on here." The baby was suffering from a severe rash and itch that *was not* responding *to any* medical treatment. Apparently the daughter's husband thought it was ridiculous to fly the baby overnight from California to New York, at such an exorbitant cost, to see a preacher; especially since none of the doctors could help her. The mother and her baby flew overnight anyway and arrived in New York in time for services at the doctor's office on Saturday afternoon. I had forgotten about the previous day's Word of Knowledge regarding itching. The baby was ministered to by the laying on of hands. The next day, on Sunday morning, the baby was completely healed! That was the reason for such great praise at the service.

The Word of Knowledge often works in concert with the Gifts of Healings, the Gift of Faith, and the Working of Miracles. In this case I don't know if the Gift of Faith to receive a miracle dropped into this mother's spirit as a result of what the grandmother told her, or if it was the mother's own personal faith. One thing is certain: this mother was not going to allow anything to deter her from bringing her child to get help from the Lord. In addition, she demonstrated tremendous faith and we know that Jesus sees our faith. The Lord *is* faithful, gracious, and full of compassion.[8]

It appears that relationship is important to God, but that distance doesn't matter.[9] In a service at a Pentecostal Holiness Church in Oklahoma, a Word of Knowledge given to me revealed the condition of an arm that was injured. The Associate pastor stood in place to receive healing for his son who was absent. After returning home his son revealed that *suddenly* his arm became healed. Upon inquiry, it was discovered that the healing took place around the same time the father stood in as a substitute for his son.

The Word of Knowledge is a fabulous Gift of the Spirit, and what a blessing it is! Desire it!

Supporting Scriptures:
The Word of Knowledge
Please read the scriptures

---

[1] Ex 4:27
[2] Ex 31:1-6
[3] Mk 6:45-50
[4] Gen 40:1-6, Mt 2:12,19,20, Acts2:17
[5] Jn 4:7-18
[6] Mt 17:24-27
[7] Acts 10:19-22, 44-48
[8] Mk 2:5, Ps 111:4
[9] Jn 4:46-53, Mt 15:22-28

Chapter Seven

THE DISCERNING OF SPIRITS

This is a marvelous and exciting Gift. The Discerning of spirits is one of the most amazing supernatural manifestations that man can experience. It is a revelation of God's knowledge that gives insight into the realm of the *spirit world* and sometimes the activities of spirits and events that are occurring in that realm, and, it enables us to distinguish whether they are Godly or evil. Through this Gift, the Holy Spirit can reveal the presence and type of a spirit being which *cannot be seen* by us. Those are the specific criteria which identify this Gift.

The Discerning of Spirits can give insight into any location in the spirit realm. This particular type of God's knowledge also extends from eternity past, covers the present, and extends into eternity future. The Holy Spirit can manifest this Gift inwardly, or through a visual manifestation. Through this Gift, God enables us to view, know or understand that which exists in the *spirit realm*, but which is concealed from us in this *natural* realm.

The reality of the spirit realm, its inhabitants and *their* activities, or *other invisible* activities in that realm, remains an area least understood by many Christians. Yet, it is an area extensively revealed throughout the Old Testament by Daniel, Elijah, certain other prophets and kings, and in the New Testament by Jesus and the apostles. With respect to evil spirits under the authority of Satan, the scriptures even go so far as to describe their ranks and levels of authority.[1]

Knowledge of the spirit realm and the activities of evil spirits are clearly understood by witches, wizards, satanic priests, occultists, and others who know *how* to operate in the spirit realm *to do evil*. However, Believers have been given *far greater power* to overcome evil spirits, their operatives, and their works. Believers have been given supernatural powers *to do tremendous good* to help themselves and others. These powers include the Holy Spirit and His Gifts, the Word of God and prayer, and the authority to use the Name of the Lord Jesus Christ. Yet, many Believers do not operate in the Power of the Holy Spirit and His Gifts. *Can we really believe God is pleased about this?* The Discerning of spirits is an essential Gift of the Spirit available to God's people. The Book of The Revelation offers invaluable descriptive evidence of the Discerning of spirits. Let's look at some evidence of this Gift from that particular Book.

The fact that the Apostle John says that he was *in the Spirit* and *saw things*, tells us immediately that the Discerning of spirits was in operation.[2] What did he see? He saw Jesus. He saw people, angelic beings and creatures, and he saw their activities. He also saw evil spirits, demons, Satan and their activities. Where did he see these beings? He saw them in Heaven, on Earth and in hell. What else did he see in the vision? He saw churches and their angel, things that *were at that time* and things that *were to come*. The Apostle John could not have seen these things with natural eyesight from here upon the Earth. It could only occur through the Discerning of spirits, by the Holy Spirit, which enabled *his spirit* to see into the spirit realm. Through the Discerning of spirits, the Holy Spirit can allow our spirit to enter into the spirit realm to see what's going on while our body remains where it is. Read the supporting scriptures about this.[3]

It is amazing that through the Discerning of spirits, John also received the Word of Knowledge, the Word of Wisdom, Prophecy, and instructions from Jesus Himself regarding things Jesus directed him to do. It is not unusual for the Word of Wisdom and the Word of Knowledge to accompany the Discerning of spirits. The entire Book of The Revelation is a great example of the Discerning of spirits in operation.

Whereas the Discerning of spirits can be manifested for any purpose God chooses, one major purpose is to enable the recognition and presence of satanic influence in a person's life so that that person may be set free of such influence *if they want to be*. Evil spirits can *influence* people, *oppress* people, and *possess* people. Jesus freed a woman who was bowed down with a spirit of infirmity for eighteen years due to *oppression* from Satan. This shows us that in some situations, evil spirits have a direct effect on certain diseases and sicknesses that affect a person's health. When this type of problem is revealed by the Discerning of spirits, and the afflicted person is set free of the demon affecting that person, his or her health is restored. Throughout the ministry of Jesus we see numerous occasions when He would cast out demons to set people free that were possessed by them. Now let's see some other scriptural examples of this spiritual Gift in operation.

In the Old Testament

In the Old Testament, we find an occasion where Israel was at war with the King of Syria. A prophet of God named Elisha was able to tell the King of Israel every move the King of Syria was going to make. The King of Syria thought there was a spy in his camp until one of his servants came and told him that there was a prophet in Israel who could tell the King of Israel everything the King of Syria said; even in his bed chamber. Obviously the Word of Knowledge and the Word of Wisdom also were at work through the prophet.

So the King of Syria sent some of his men to find out where Elisha was staying. They reported back that Elisha was staying in a city called Dothan. The King of Syria then, at night, dispatched a great army with horses and chariots to surround the city. Early the next morning, Elisha's servant awoke and went outside. What he saw gave him big time fear. He saw that a great Syrian army of horses and chariots had surrounded the city. In fear, he ran back to Elisha and told him what he saw. Then in essence he asked Elisha, "*Now* what are we going to do?" Elisha simply maintained his cool and told his servant, "Fear not! Those with us *are more* than those with them."

Elisha knew that he was protected by invisible forces which were present, but in the spirit realm. By the way, angels can protect you too, if you know how to activate them with the Word of God. Then Elisha prayed and asked the Lord to open the eyes of the young man that he might see. The *Discerning of spirits* manifested when the Lord opened the *spiritual* eyes of the young man for him to see into the spirit realm. What did he see? He saw that the mountain was full of horses and chariots round about Elisha.[4] The Gift of the Discerning of spirits can enable us to see in the spirit realm that which we cannot penetrate with our natural eyesight. It can also *give us information* about spirit beings in that realm, their activities, as well as *other activities* occurring in that realm which may affect us in this realm.

In the Earthly Life and Ministry of Jesus Christ

During the earthly life and ministry of Jesus, a man brought his son to the disciples of Jesus for help because his son was a lunatic. The boy was possessed with a devil that often threw him into fire, and often into water. Since the disciples could not cast the devil out, the father took his son to Jesus. Here's where the Holy Spirit comes into play. He not only gives Jesus the power to cast that devil out, but by *the Discerning of spirits*, the Holy Spirit also reveals to Jesus the type of spirit possessing the boy. It was a foul, unclean, dumb and deaf spirit that caused the boy to foam at the mouth and gnash his teeth. Jesus cast the spirit out of the boy. [5]

On another occasion, when Jesus was on his way to Jerusalem just prior to going to the cross, He told His disciples the things that were going to happen to Him; that He was going to suffer reproach, humiliation, and ultimately be put to death. Jesus knew *this had* to happen. But His disciple Peter didn't, and said to Jesus, "Be it far from thee Lord, *this shall not* be unto thee!" Then Jesus responded, "Get thee behind me, Satan: for thou savourest not the things that be of God, but the things that be of men."[6]

Here's what's going on. Peter loved Jesus and Jesus loved him. There is no way that Jesus would believe Peter was Satan! On the natural level, Peter didn't want anything to happen to Jesus and on the spiritual level he couldn't understand why Jesus had to suffer, go to the cross, die, and be raised again the third day! But by the Discerning of spirits, Jesus knew that the thoughts and actions of Peter were *under the influence* of an evil power, and that it was Satan himself influencing Peter. Jesus was actually speaking to Satan, not Peter. A similar situation like this occurred in the Early Church as we shall see next.

In the Early Church

The Apostle Paul and a company of others were on their way to pray when they were met by a young girl who was possessed by a spirit of divination. She brought her masters much financial gain with her ability in fortune-telling, claiming to tell future events and discover hidden knowledge. She kept following Paul and those with him around, and kept on claiming, "These men are servants of the Most High God." After several days of doing this, Paul recognized *by the Discerning of spirits* that she was controlled by an evil spirit. Now, notice what Paul did. He spoke to the spirit! Not to the girl, but *to the spirit* that was controlling the girl, and commanded it to come out of her in the Name of Jesus Christ. The spirit came out, and she could no longer do the things she could previously do. Of course, this enraged her master who could no longer get financial profit from the activities that she could previously do. He even went so far as to bring serious charges against Paul that caused him to be beaten and put in jail.[7]

There's a lesson here for us to learn. The Gift of the Discerning of spirits by the Holy Spirit *is not* a "gift of discernment" which some people claim *they* have. Scripturally, there is no such thing as a "gift of discernment." The so called "gift of discernment" is one of the greatest ways the Discerning of spirits is falsely claimed and then misused and abused. This is done by judging and finding faults in other people *and linking* those humanly perceived faults to some kind of a demon. Doing this is error! Never engage in this kind of "spiritual" nonsense and don't allow yourself to become a victim of someone else who does. Scripture tells us to judge ourselves and get the beam of fault out of our own eye first before finding fault in someone else. Neither Jesus nor Paul found fault with *the person*. They only dealt with *the spirit* exerting its influence upon the person *when* it was revealed to them by the Holy Spirit.

In the Life and Ministry of the Author

I think you will find this next example of the Discerning of spirits to be pretty profound. It occurred *before* I became a minister of the Gospel. It involved a medical doctor, who at the time of the incident, I thought was under severe demonic influence. But I *now* know that he was demon *possessed*. At *that* time, I was fairly knowledgeable of scriptures *and* was baptized in the Holy Spirit. But I knew *nothing* about His spiritual Gifts! However, they still *did* manifest through me. Before you knew what they were, I wouldn't be surprised if some of the Gifts of the Spirit may have operated through you, too. But you never knew it, or you never knew what it was. Hopefully, after reading this book, you will know. Here's what happened.

One Sunday morning following church service, a group of Believers came to tell me about a medical doctor in the local area who was sleeping and living out of a car. Because of my professional background, *they* felt that I was the perfect one to talk to him, find out what was going on, and help him to get his life turned around. But not personally knowing the doctor, I wasn't too enthusiastic about getting involved!

The next day, Monday, about 6:00 P.M., we received a telephone call from the same Believers telling us where the doctor and his car were, and requesting that my wife and I go to see him. My wife floated the possibility to me that perhaps we would have to bring him home so he would have a place to stay for awhile. My response was immediate and definite: no way! I was willing to provide him a hotel room for a week or so, but not my home.

We located the car and found him asleep inside. The car was dirty inside and packed with worn clothes, old shoes, cooking utensils, some family pictures, and other paraphernalia. After introducing ourselves, we discovered that he had not eaten all day so we took him across the street to a restaurant for dinner. Now here is where my first hair-raising experience with an evil spirit began.

While waiting for the waitress to bring our meals, this doctor looked at me with what seemed to be *unnatural* piercing eyes and started speaking out in a weird voice saying, "Eye-e, am the Way;" meaning *he* was "the Way" to salvation. This he said twice and we ignored him. But the third time he said this I became annoyed, grieved in my spirit and blurted out in a firm voice, "No, *you're not* the Way. *Jesus is* the *Way*." Then He *astounded* me with his response saying, "But your heart, 'Doc-tor' Givens". This was weird, and this was shocking because I had never met nor seen this man before in my life. Yet, *he* knew I had had a heart condition a year or so earlier before being supernaturally healed by God.

Instantly, within a moment of a split second, the Holy Spirit manifested Himself. If this has never happened to you it may be difficult to understand. But suddenly from the core and essence of my being, I *knew all things* related to what was happening. I knew a demon was speaking to me and not a man. I knew *he* knew about my past. I knew he was about to speak cursing words which could affect my heart. I knew he had to be immediately shut up and not speak a word. I also knew he would not listen to words of normal persuasion. Then a supernatural force moved through my belly area and I began to speak with great force a litany of scriptures while staring him straight in the eyes. "No Satan, you're a liar. I belong to the Most High God. Jesus is my Lord and by His stripes I am healed. I'm covered by the Blood of the Lamb. No evil weapon formed against me shall prosper!" Then I *distinctly* remember saying, "At the Name of Jesus every knee *must* bow, now *you* bow your knee to the Name of Jesus *and shut up!*"[8] This all came out without me thinking or deciding what to say. It became very loud in there. People stopped eating and were looking at us! I didn't know *what* to expect.

What happened next *absolutely* amazed me. This demon possessed man looked at me, looked down at the table, closed his eyes, then literally and deliberately very *slowly* bowed his head low, *and shut up!* To see *that*, was astounding.

I *now* know that my victory was due to the Power of the Holy Spirit, the Discerning of spirits, the Word of Knowledge, and the power of the spoken Word of God. The demon involved is called a familiar spirit. Nothing like *that* had ever happened to me before, nor has it happened since.

On several other occasions however, the Holy Spirit has allowed me, through the Discerning of spirits, to actually see evil spirits in the spirit realm. On one particular occasion, *during a time of prayer*, an evil spirit and his activities were seen. His name and purpose were revealed to me. His purpose was to create financial confusion. Interestingly enough, though I made no connection at the time, this happened during the time of the great American Savings and Loan scandal which occurred during the late nineteen eighties. With the crazy things going on around us today, it is good to know that the Holy Spirit and His Gifts can help us by revealing some of the causes for the detrimental events that we see going on. We can then direct *our* prayer activities more specifically and effectively.

The Discerning of Spirits and Sensory Perceptions

Let me share with you another aspect about the Discerning of spirits that you may find interesting. The sensory perceptions that we have, like the ability to see, hear, smell, and so forth, can *also* be experienced in the spirit realm. Let me give you a *scriptural example* of what I'm talking about. It involves the ability to *hear* in the spiritual realm.

During the reign of a king in Israel named Ahab, God sent a drought and great famine upon the land because of wickedness and the people's worship of a false god named Baal; to whom four hundred and fifty *false* prophets were loyal. So a prophet of God named Elijah challenged the false prophets as to who *the real* God was: theirs, or Elijah's. Both camps agreed to offer a young calf as a sacrifice to their god and pray to him to reveal himself by fire.

For hours the prophets of Baal called on their god, leaped up and down on the altar, yelled, and cut themselves with knives until they profusely spilled blood. Yet nothing happened. Later in the evening, Elijah prayed and Jehovah, the Almighty God, was the One who spectacularly answered by fire in response to his prayer. After proving that his God reigned, and after slaying all of the false prophets of Baal, Elijah then went to see King Ahab. Now here's where we're going to see that the Discerning of spirits can be associated with sensory perception, and the Word of Wisdom also.

Elijah went to see Ahab because God had previously spoken to him and instructed him to go and tell Ahab that He was going to send rain upon the Earth to end the long drought. That was a Word of Wisdom. Now watch *the kind* of Discerning of spirits that occurred when Elijah went to see Ahab. Elijah said to Ahab, "Get thee up, eat, and drink; for there is *a sound* of abundance of rain." *Sound* is a *sensory perception* of something you hear! Now let me ask you a question. How on earth could Elijah hear rain, when at the particular moment he was speaking it was a clear day outside without even a cloud in the sky? In the natural, he couldn't!

What he heard was the a*ctivity of rain in the invisible spirit realm* by the Discerning of spirits, *before* the rain actually occurred in this natural *Earth realm*. This is a Word of Wisdom *again*, along *with* the Discerning of spirits since a great rain did occur later.

Various types of sensory perceptions, like those which we experience here on earth, can also be experienced in the spirit realm by the Discerning of spirits *as the Holy Spirit wills.*[9] From experience, I can tell you that if the Holy Spirit through the Discerning of spirits ever opens your ears to hear Heavenly music, you will hear musical sounds you have never heard before that is *too gorgeous to describe*. This is consistent with scripture that tells us that eyes have not seen, nor ear heard the things that God has prepared for those who love Him. But God reveals them to us by the Spirit.[10] The Holy Spirit, through the Discerning of spirits, can reveal to us sensory perceptions in the spirit realm related to seeing, smelling, touching, and tasting as well as hearing.

Non Believers Cannot Cast Out Devils

Since the Discerning of spirits can expose the presence or influence of devils, it's good to know that devils can be cast out of someone possessed with them by the Power of the Holy Spirit in the Name of Jesus Christ if that person *wants to be set free.* [11] But as we're now going to see, not everybody can cast a devil out of a possessed person.

During the Early Church era, there was a certain Jewish chief priest named Sceva who had seven sons. On a certain occasion they were trying to cast an evil spirit out of someone using the Name of the Lord Jesus. This is what they said when they were trying to cast the evil spirit out. "We adjure you by Jesus *whom Paul preacheth.*" The evil spirit answered them and said, "Jesus I know, and Paul I know: *but who are ye?*"[12] That tells us something important that we need to know when dealing directly with evil spirits. It is this: all evil spirits know exactly who Jesus Christ is, and they know of the supremacy of His Name. They also know who has the authority to use His Name, and they know *who doesn't.* From what happened next, it's obvious that none of these men personally knew Jesus, didn't have the right to use His Name, and had no access to the Holy Spirit. Hence they had no power of God. Therefore, they couldn't possibly do what they were trying to do because they didn't meet the requirements for the ability to do so. Look what happened.

The man who had the evil spirit leaped on them, overcame them, and prevailed against them to such an extent that they all ran out of the man's house *naked* and *wounded.* This proves that some evil spirits possessing a person can have supernatural strength *far greater* than human strength and can literally inflict enough physical violence to overcome several people. But regardless of their strength, ability, or numbers, all evil spirits are subject to, absolutely must and do obey commands spoken to them by *any* Believer who uses the authority, the faith, and the power to use the Name of Jesus Christ to cast them out. *Unbelievers cannot cast out devils because they have neither the authority nor power to do so.* However, there's *another* reason *why* unbelievers cannot cast out devils and Jesus Himself explains it to us.

Jesus was accused of casting out devils by the prince of devils called Beelzebub.[13] Jesus made it clear that *that* couldn't be the case because it would mean that Satan was acting against himself. In other words, Satan, who is the commanding chief of all demon spirits, wouldn't allow someone in his own kingdom to cast a devil out of a person when *all devils* need to possess an earthly physical body in order to exert *maximum* evil influence on behalf of Satan. If they can't possess a human body, which is their preference, they will even settle for a pig or other animal.[14] So the question then, is what *does this* have to do with *unbelievers'* inability to cast out devils? Here's the answer.

Satan controls his kingdom through his loyal demon spirits, also called devils. The greatest achievement of devils occurs when they possess and control a human being. Satan certainly is not going to give a human being that *does not* belong to Jesus, and therefore *is not in the Kingdom of God*, the authority to cast any devil *out* of another person who *is in his* kingdom and under the control of one of his loyal demons. If he did allow such a thing to happen, Satan would be dividing and weakening his own kingdom just as Jesus said. After all, a demon possessing a person is carrying out Satan's objective to deceive, manipulate, and then steal, kill, or eventually destroy the same person he has possessed and used; a person that God had created! This is *the other reason why* unbelievers *cannot* cast out devils.

The powers that can effect the beings and activities of the spirit realm are the Holy Spirit, the Name of Jesus, the Word of God, and the Blood of the Lamb. These powers are carried out through prayer. Should the Holy Spirit *will* to manifest the Discerning of spirits through you, you will find it to be a thrilling and awesome experience.

A Time To Refresh

I hope you will agree that the Holy Spirit has given us a lot of insight and information thus far. We have discovered that the Lord Jesus Christ is the Master Connection between the Holy Spirit and His supernatural spiritual Gifts. We have seen how the Holy Spirit helps us on both personal *and* spiritual levels. We have obtained deep insight into the three wonderful Gifts of God's Divine Revelation Knowledge. From the Discerning of spirits we've been made aware of the invisible spirit realm, and the ability to see spirit beings and their activities in that realm. There's a whole lot more He has in store for us! So, perhaps this is a good time to just relax, meditate on what you have received, and meditate on the scriptures that support what you have read.

Don't forget to pray, and expect the Holy Spirit to give you even greater understanding consistent with God's Word. We're going to continue next with an in depth look at the marvelous and astounding supernatural Gifts of God's Divine Power and Ability. These are the Working of Miracles, the Gift of Faith, and the Gifts of Healings.

Supporting Scriptures:
The Discerning of spirits
Please read the scriptures

---

[1] Eph 6:12
[2] Rev 1:10
[3] Rev 1-22:16
[4] 2 Ki 6:8-17
[5] Mk 9:14-29
[6] Mt 16:21-23
[7] Acts 16:16-24
[8] Jn 8:44, I Pet 2:24, Is 53:4,5, Rev 12:11, Is 54:17, Phil 2:9,10
[9] 1 Ki 18: 1, 20-40, 41-45
[10] 1 Cor 2:9,10
[11] Col 2:15, Phil 2:9-11, Jn 14:13
[12] Acts 19:13-17, 16:18, Phil 2:9,10,11
[13] Mt 12:24-26,
[14] Mk 5:9-13, Mt 8:28-32

THE GIFTS OF DIVINE POWER AND ABILITY

Now that we have covered the Gifts of Divine Revelation Knowledge, let's move on to give attention to God's supernatural Gifts that demonstrate His Divine Power and Ability. These are The Gift of Faith, The Gifts of Healings, and The Working of Miracles. These Gifts are absolutely astounding. You will enjoy learning about them and be even more pleased to discover that they can operate through *you too*, as the Holy Spirit wills. We'll look at The Gift of Faith first.

CHAPTER EIGHT

THE GIFT OF FAITH

The faith of God reveals His absolute phenomenal ability. With His awesome faith He framed the world by His Word, and the things which we see were not made of things that were. In other words, the physical material that He needed to create the Earth didn't even exist. With *His* faith, He raised Jesus from the dead by the Holy Spirit. This is the kind of faith He can manifest through us by the Holy Spirit. It is called the Gift of Faith.[1]

Scripture tells us that everyone is given the measure, a portion, or an amount of faith. We also know that there are different *kinds* of faith. There's "saving faith," which enables someone to receive eternal salvation by grace from God. There's faith, which is one of the fruit of the spirit that refers to faithfulness. We also know that we pray by faith.[2]

Faith is a law that incorporates words. Words spoken in faith can produce miracles. Every miracle God produced is a result of words He *spoke*, *said*, or *called* to bring something into being. God speaks things into existence by calling things *that are not as though they were,* and they become reality. This is how He brought the worlds into existence.

The Lord Jesus Christ tells us in scripture that we too can speak words of faith and have miracles occur.[3]

But *The Gift of Faith* is different. The Gift of Faith is a supernatural manifestation of God working through a person! It is so unique, so awesome, and so tremendous that it can only be manifested by the Holy Spirit as He wills, when and where He wills, and through whom He Wills. Through the Gift of Faith, *the Holy Spirit* provides absolute and complete *certainty* that when you *speak or act on what you believe God to do,* what you believe will occur. The Gift of Faith always results in a Divine Intervention by God. These criteria identify this Gift.

In the Old Testament

In the Old Testament, one of many prophets that all lived together went to their leader Elisha and told him that the place where they were staying was too small. So they all went over to the Jordan River to cut down trees to make beams large enough to build another dwelling.

One of the prophets *borrowed* an axe. Unfortunately, while cutting down a tree the axe head fell off into the water and was lost. The young prophet was so worried that he went to Elisha to tell him the problem. Elisha went to the spot where the incident happened, cut down a stick, and threw it into the water where the axe head sank. The axe head *floated* to the top of the water! The young prophet who lost it happily retrieved it.[4] Now that was a "big time" miracle. *But it had to be the Gift of Faith* working through Elisha to cause God to perform this miracle because nobody, without special supernatural faith given by the Holy Spirit, could believe that such a miracle could even be possible. Another sensational example of the Gift of Faith in action is seen in the life of King David when he was a lad. Here's the background.

The King of Israel, Saul, and his armies were set to do battle against people called the Philistines, and their army.

The armies were on opposite sides of two hills separated by a valley. The Philistines had in their camp a mighty, powerful giant warrior that was named Goliath. He was over eight feet tall, and was one fearsome sight to behold when he was in full battle dress. He wore a helmet of brass, a coat weighing four hundred sixty eight pounds made of metal plates of brass, brass armor protecting the shins of his legs, carried a spear with a head weighing fifty six pounds, and then, had someone bearing *a protective shield that went in front of him* during battle![5] This guy appeared to have *everything* going for him that would make him totally unbeatable in battle.

Goliath called out to the armies of Israel and in essence challenged them to send out one man to do battle with only him, man to man, *one on one*. The people represented by the loser would be servants to the people of the victor. Scripture tells us that when King Saul and all Israel heard the words of Goliath, they were *greatly* afraid; in other words, they were beaten down, discouraged, and terrified. Goliath did this for forty days.[6] But watch this!

Young David was the shepherd for his father's sheep. One morning, in obedience to his father, he left the sheep to take food to his brothers who were stationed on the battle line for war against the Philistines. As David arrived at his brothers' position, the giant Goliath appeared. The men of Israel in the area were so terrified that they all ran away.[7]

Meanwhile, David kept asking the men near him what would be done for the man who killed this Philistine and remove the reproach from Israel. Word got back to King Saul about David's questioning and Saul sent for him.[8] When Saul saw David he said, "You're not able to go out against this Philistine and fight him. You're only a boy, and he has been a fighting *man* since his youth."[9]

But from the scriptural passage we discover that the Gift of Faith had operated through David on at least two *previous* occasions, and he was victorious. David stated that when a lion or bear carried off his sheep, he went after it and took the sheep from the mouth of the attacker. And when the animal *turned on him*, he seized it by the hair, struck it, and killed it. That's not normal faith! No person would dare engage a bear and lion in this manner. That's special faith given by the Holy Spirit of God, called the Gift of Faith.[10] And now, we're going to see the Gift of Faith operating through David again as he engages in combat with Goliath. But first, here's some piercing insight the Holy Spirit wants us to have.

As they were approaching each other for mortal combat, notice what Goliath said, then notice what David said in reply. Big bad Goliath said, "Come to me and I will give your flesh to the fowls of the air, and to the wild beast of the Earth." In other words, Goliath was so confident in *his* might, power, ability, armor, and weapons, that he just knew he would cut David up in such a devastating way that the wild animals would eat up the remains of his flesh.[11]

Now listen to what David said when he replied to Goliath! "You come to me with a sword, and with a spear, and with a shield: but I come to you in the Name of the Lord of hosts, the God of the armies of Israel. This day *the Lord* will deliver you into *my* hands." In essence David was saying, "You're coming to me in all of the confidence you have in *your ability*, but I'm coming to you in all of the confidence I have in *God's ability*. After *the Lord* puts you into my hands, I'm going to cut your head off, and do to you what you said you were going to do to me." Now look at the main reason *why* David said he's going to do this: "That all the Earth may know there is a God in Israel."

With great trust in God, and knowing that he had a covenant with God, David *runs towards* the giant Goliath, whom everyone else *was running from*, and kills the giant by hitting him in the forehead with a stone that he threw from his slingshot.[12]

Here are the keys to David's victory. First, whereas Goliath had absolute confidence in *his own* physical, mental, material, and combat ability, David had absolute and total confidence in God's ability and his covenant *with* God. Goliath depended upon *his own ability*. David depended upon *God's ability* and his *covenant* with God. Secondly, Goliath wanted the victory for himself and his people, whereas David wanted the victory so that *everybody would know that there is a God!* Goliath's *motives* were for himself and his people. David's *motives* were for God's glory; the spoils of the victory were merely a by-product. [A]

The magnificent insight that the Holy Spirit wants us to receive seems to be this: when confronted with a seemingly impossible situation *in the natural*, we must place total and absolute confidence, trust, and belief in God's ability, and we must fervently long *to see God* revealed, exalted, and glorified *by the victory*. I have found from experience that these two things seem to put me into position for the Holy Spirit, as He wills, to *supernaturally* drop into my heart *an absolute knowing* that He *will* overcome the problem, right then. This is the way I have experienced the awesome Gift of Faith in action.

[A] **For expanded insight on this passage of scripture and the powerful effect it can have on us personally, see the subject: A Realization and Understanding of Great Value, page 106.**

In the Earthly Life and Ministry of Jesus Christ

In the earthly life and ministry of Jesus Christ, we see an interesting example of the Gift of Faith in operation which validates the exact same understanding that inspired David: *Covenant Rights!* Let's set the stage surrounding this example.

Jesus was teaching in a synagogue on the Sabbath day. There was a woman there who had a spirit of infirmity; a spirit of infirmity is a demon that causes sickness, and it usually needs to be cast out before healing can occur. The spirit of infirmity in this woman was so severe that she was bent forward, and of *her own* power and ability she absolutely could not straighten herself up. By the Discerning of spirits Jesus knew that it was Satan who had her bound by a spirit of infirmity. By a Word of Knowledge, Jesus also knew that she had suffered in this condition for eighteen years! Obviously He was moved with compassion, but it is *how* He dealt with this situation that is so revealing and informative.[13]

By the Holy Spirit, whom Jesus sometimes referred to as the "finger of God,"[14] He could have cast that spirit of infirmity out and then commanded her to be healed! But He didn't do that. Jesus knew that this woman had *covenant rights* with God since she was a daughter of Abraham. Therefore He *knew* she had *a right* to be healed, and I believe the Gift of Faith was manifested through Him accordingly. Because of her covenant with God, He simply *told her* that she was loosed from her infirmity. *Then*, even without casting the demon out that caused the problem, He laid His hand upon her and she was immediately healed! Jesus must have received the Gift of Faith to believe that God would perform this healing miracle because He didn't even bother to first cast the demon out.

In this example we see *several* results from the Gifts of the Spirit being in operation. This is not uncommon. But when the Gift of Faith is in operation, two things are *always common*. First, the manifestation of the Gift of Faith always brings forth a direct intervention by God into the situation, often resulting in a miracle. Secondly, God is always *revealed and glorified.*

Here's another occasion when the Gift of Faith was manifested through Jesus. Jesus entered into a synogue on a Sabbath day to teach, and a man with a withered right hand was there. The religious leaders of the day observed a law forbidding anyone from doing work on the Sabbath. This included doing good things like healing people. The religious leaders watched Jesus very carefully to see if He would break their law so that they could accuse Him. But Jesus had sized them up. He knew how they thought and He knew what they were up to. He also knew that the Sabbath was made for rest, blessings, and for *the benefit of man*, not *man* for t*he benefit of rituals* on the Sabbath.[15]

Jesus desired to demonstrate the love and grace of God even on the Sabbath! Here's where the Holy Spirit helped Him. He manifested to Jesus supernatural faith to believe that God would perform a mighty miracle for this man. By the Gift of Faith, Jesus told this man to stretch forth his hand. Without knowing why, the man obeyed, stretched forth his withered right hand, and it was made whole just like the other hand.[16] This is a prime example of the Holy Spirit manifesting the Gift of Faith, and God responding by performing a miracle. Now again, you might say, "Yeah but that was Jesus, the Son of God." True! But remember, Jesus set aside *all* of His *Godly* attributes while He lived and ministered here upon the Earth.[17] He depended totally upon the Holy Spirit *then*, as He wants you and me to do *now*. The Holy Spirit desires to work *today* through us, just as He worked *then*, through Jesus.

In the Early Church

From the Early Church era, we notice that the Gift of Faith *may sometimes* involve more than one person when a miracle from God is needed. Let's look at an example from scripture to describe what I mean.

We find in the Book of the Acts that Peter and John were going into the Temple to pray. There was a man who lay at the Gate daily that was born lame. Today we'd call the man a helpless invalid. He begged for charitable gifts called alms. The lame man saw Peter and John and asked *them* for alms. Now watch the reaction of Peter. He gazed at the lame man and boldly said, "Look on us." He was commanding the man to pay attention to what he was going to say. The scriptures say that the lame man gave heed to them expecting to receive *something* from them.[18] Now let's stop a moment and see what's going on here.

Knowing that he didn't have any money on him, the Gift of Faith must have dropped into Peter's spirit that God would perform a miracle for this man or else he wouldn't have so boldly drawn the man's attention to what he was going to say. In other words, the Holy Spirit dropped this special supernatural faith into Peter's spirit for him to believe that God would perform a miracle to make this cripple man whole, and thereby *glorify* the Name of Jesus Christ.

Remember now, Peter had the lame man's attention. The Holy Spirit *must* have *also* dropped the Gift of Faith into this invalid man's heart that *he* was going to get *something great*. What ever it was, he was going to take it! Then Peter, full of supernatural faith by the Holy Spirit acted on it. In essence Peter said, "Man I don't have any money, but I'm going to give you what I *do* have." What did Peter *know* he had? He *knew* he had the right to use the Name of Jesus Christ and he had *absolute confidence* that whatever he commanded to be done in *that* Name, Jesus would do it.[19] That's the mighty Gift of Faith in action. So, he commanded the cripple man to stand up and walk in the Name of Jesus Christ. Then he put action to his faith in that Name by grabbing the man by the hand and lifting him up to walk. God immediately performed the miracle. The man's feet and ankle bones received strength. He leaped up, stood, then went walking and leaping into the Temple with Peter and John, *praising God.* That was the Gift of Faith operating through Peter for God to perform a miracle. But how did the Gift of Faith operate through the lame man to *receive* the miracle? Peter himself explains it in the scripture.

When all of the people saw the lame man walking, they wondered what happened. Peter told them that God *had glorified* His Son Jesus Christ. Then Peter told them *how* the Gift of Faith operated through the cripple man to help him to receive his miracle. Peter in essence said to them, "And His Name, meaning the Name of Jesus Christ, through special faith in His Name hath made this man strong, whom you see and know: yes, *the special faith given by Jesus* which the cripple man received, has given him this perfect soundness." Faith given by Jesus is the supernatural Gift of Faith manifested by the Holy Spirit. So, the cripple man's miracle was a result of the Gift of Faith operating through both Peter and the cripple man, and the six powerful words, *"In the Name of Jesus Christ,"* spoken by Peter.

In the Life and Ministry of the Author

As we have seen, the Gift of Faith often works in combination with other Gifts of the Spirit. This is especially true with The Word of Knowledge. The Holy Spirit may reveal through a Word of Knowledge that someone is harassed by a bad habit and wants it broken. The Discerning of spirits may reveal possession with an evil spirit, and identify the type of demon involved. Then it can be cast out by a Believer with sufficient faith and power if the person desires to be set free. Using two different real life examples, we're now going to see the difference between faith, presumption, and the Gift of Faith.

Many years ago, I was ministering at a church service in the Caribbean. The Gifts of Healings were flowing profusely and miracles were happening. Suddenly, a short man who was bent over with a hump back bolted out of a pew to my left, ran up the center isle, and kicked me full force where it's not nice to kick men. Apparently, I was well protected by the anointing because I felt absolutely no pain and had no after affects. Four men quickly grabbed this imp-ape looking human, threw him to the floor and held him down. He was obviously demon possessed and he was mad! For about five minutes, while he was being held down, I did everything I knew to do to cast that devil out of him in the Name of Jesus. *Nothing* happened!

Now, I wouldn't be telling you the truth if I didn't tell you that at *that* point my faith was *badly* shaken. After the service, I hurried back to the hotel with tears in my eyes, disillusioned, upset at my inability to cast that devil out, and to be honest with you, I was even a little bit upset with the Lord. It was a long night of prayer. What happened! Now,

I know.

It was my lack of understanding and faith. The Holy Spirit didn't give me the Discerning of spirits regarding this character, nor did He *instruct me* to cast that demon out, nor did He *lead me* to cast that devil out, nor did I have the faith, nor Gift of Faith, to cast that devil out. It was me on my own, who decided to cast that devil out. The Holy Spirit *never gave me the authority* to cast that devil out, *nor did He give me the power*. The decision was mine and the results were mine. I was presumptuous. Can't blame God.

All evil spirits are subject to obey the Name of Jesus Christ. However, sometimes we simply don't have the level of faith necessary to expel the demon.[20] Likewise, some people *don't want* a demon to go! Plus, there are other factors. Therefore, never be presumptuous; *especially* if you have *not yet* received the Baptism with the Holy Spirit.[B]

Now let's contrast *this* experience where *my personal faith* was not sufficient to bring forth good results, compared to an experience where the Gift of Faith *did* manifest and brought forth magnificent results. In both examples proper scriptural procedures were followed. But in one case the Gift of Faith manifested and was followed by a marvelous miracle, even though a popular *faith* principle espoused by many today *would appear* to be violated *if it is not* fully understood.

The Holy Spirit loves to glorify the Lord Jesus Christ in the fullness of His love, His grace, and His power. So let me set the scene for you where the Holy Spirit through a Word of Knowledge identified *one* condition, then later manifested the Gift of Faith which resulted in a wonderful miracle done by God to correct *another* condition.

[B] **See Discerning of spirits, Page 86 "sons of Sceva."**

This experience happened to me in Denver, Colorado while ministering at a small, store front Pentecostal church on a Wednesday night. The congregation of about twenty-five people was loudly singing and praising God with cymbals and tambourines like you can't believe. The pastor was non-flamboyant, gentle, and had the most beautiful spirit that you can imagine. *These* Believers, though few in number, truly revered the Lord, and meant business. I was *delighted* to be praising God with them. Following the ministry of the Word, the Holy Spirit led me to minister with the Gifts of the Spirit. Here's how a Word of Knowledge, followed later by the Gift of Faith, resulted in a beautiful miracle from God.

The Holy Spirit revealed to me through a Word of Knowledge that He wanted to heal someone who had pain in both ankles. An elderly woman in her early eighties hobbled forth. I knelt down on one knee and dealt with the pain in her ankles with Words of God and the Name of Jesus Christ. As I arose to my feet, my eyes *were led* to her eyes which looked opaque and strange. I asked, "What's wrong with your eyes, sister?" Four or five people in the congregation yelled out, "She's blind!"

After I heard that, the Holy Spirit instructed me to deal with her eyes. I then said to the congregation, "Is *that* so! Well, let's just see what the Lord is going to do about it." I then laid my left hand upon her eyes and through commands dealt with every component of the eyes including the nerves and visual center of the brain. I commanded her to see, in the Name of Jesus Christ. I then asked her if she *could* see. *"No,"* was her answer. Nothing happened, *that we could tell!* No problem, I just instructed the congregation to continue thanking Jesus for her eyesight, never doubt, but continue to believe God for her healing. I also reminded them that Jesus was the Healer, *not me!*

At my hotel the following morning, I received a phone call from a lady exclaiming, "Mother can see, mother can see, but she sees two of everything." Immediately, the Holy Spirit brought to my attention a passage of scripture where Jesus laid hands on a blind man. The blind man received his sight, but he said he saw as trees; meaning in twos, or double. Scripture then says that Jesus laid His hands upon the man *again!* Then the man saw perfectly.[21] So, I had a decision to make. Do I follow the teaching of men which says, and properly so, that when you lay hands on someone for healing *by faith* you only do it once? Or, do I follow the example set by Jesus in a similar circumstance as *this* was! No contest. I said, "Come get me and take me to her." It was at this point that the Gift of Faith dropped into my spirit for her to receive total recovery of her eyesight. They picked me up, took me to her, and I laid my hands upon her *again* and commanded natural sight to occur in the Name of Jesus Christ. The Lord immediately gave her perfect eyesight.

The reason this was proper to do is that I did not previously lay hands on her and *pray to God* for her to receive healing for blindness *by faith*. Instead, I laid hands on her to demand *in the Name of Jesus Christ* that she see.[C] The Lord gave her perfect eyesight when I did *this* again. What a glorious miracle God performed!

Here's the contrast between this experience and the previous experience where I, *on my own*, decided to cast a devil out. In this case, the Holy Spirit *brought this lady to me* through a Word of Knowledge. The Holy Spirit *led* me to look at her eyes and to inquire about them. The Holy Spirit *instructed* me *to demand* that she see by the faith that I

[C] **See Power: How we Release the power Page 166**

had in *the Name of Jesus*. The Holy Spirit *placed* the Gift of Faith for her miracle into my spirit. The lesson and principle for us is this: follow the leading of the Holy Spirit and be consistent with the scriptures.

A Realization and Understanding of Great Value

Let me share with you something that I have learned from experience about the Gift of Faith that may be of value to you also. It relates to *personal belief* in God and having a *covenant* with Him. I first realized this connection with the Gift of Faith while studying *the attitude* of David when he went up against Goliath. The Gift of Faith operates only at the will of the Holy Spirit. But I've noticed that when this Gift *has* operated through me, it has been at those times when my confidence in God was like that of David's. So let's examine this a little further.

When we study the passage of scripture related to David and Goliath, we discover from David's own words some fascinating information about the understanding *he had* regarding God, his *belief* in God, and *the covenant he had* with God. This was essential to David, and it has proven to be essential to me. Let's look at it.

First of all, regardless of the exploit, David's total acknowledgement is all about what God has done. Not about what David has done, but about what God has done and *his dependence* upon God. He explains the process, and tells *how* God used him, but *the credit* for the outcome *all* went to God.[22] King Saul was concerned that David was out of his league going up against Goliath. But listen to what David said. "*The Lord* that delivered me out of the paw of the lion, and out of the paw of the bear, *He* will deliver me out of the hand of this Philistine!" Not *can* deliver me, but *will* deliver me! I believe the "*will* deliver me" part is the Gift of Faith. But notice his total confidence and trust in the Lord. David believed that the battle was the Lord's, *not his*! And he said so![23] Who in the world can beat God? Nobody! And David *knew* this. The question then, becomes how can David have such great confidence? Again, through *his own words* he gives us the clue. And here it is.

When David was among the men that became terrified and ran away when they saw Goliath, David asked them an *all telling* question, "Who is this *uncircumcised* Philistine, that *he* should defy *the armies* of the *living God?*" There's the key to his confidence: an uncircumcised Philistine, *versus* a living God. Here's why it's the key.

In the Old Testament, Israelites like David had a covenant with the Almighty living God that was sealed by the blood of animals. The *sign* of that covenant, mandated by God, was circumcision for all Israelite males. A covenant is basically an agreement between two parties which in effect says, "I'm totally on your side and you're totally on mine in all things. What I have belongs to you, and what you have belongs to me. Therefore, my battle is your battle." In this case the covenant was between God and Israel. David knew, *being an Israelite*, that he too was included in that covenant with God.[24] David also knew that Goliath was an *uncircumcised* male. Therefore he was *without* a covenant with the Almighty living God, and although Goliath may not have known it, David knew *and believed* there was no way Goliath could defeat him and God *together*. David had to have believed that *with* God *nothing* was impossible. His understanding of his covenant with God, along with his previous experiences, appears to be why David had such great confidence that he could go up against Goliath and prevail. And he did!

Therefore, with respect to my own experiences with the Gift of Faith, I simply realize and understand that because I belong to the Lord Jesus Christ, God's *covenant* with me is far greater than the covenant that David had because mine is based upon the *righteousness* and *grace* of God, and it is *sealed by the blood of Jesus* on my behalf. Mine is also based upon better promises.[25] This realization and understanding has been of great value to me. I have discovered that as He wills, the Holy Spirit simply supercharges my confidence and faith in God's ability, and His covenant with me, by dropping the Gift of Faith into my spirit so that *I know* He will do what I ask of Him. The Holy Spirit *knows* that I want God only, to get the glory. By the way, *you* can have this exact same covenant with God by accepting Jesus Christ as your personal Savior.

The Gift of Faith can Operate Through You

From the opening paragraph of this chapter you will recall hearing me say that the Gift of Faith can operate through us. This means through you, too. I believe the Holy Spirit would have me to share an incident with you that will verify this fact. When my mother-in-law was first married, she was observing her husband doing some car repair in the yard. He was underneath the car which was propped up with jacks when suddenly the jacks collapsed and the car fell upon him. She immediately ran to the car, picked it up off of her husband, and moved it enough to save his life.

Now, there may be some who would say that her response was because of an adrenalin rush; which is a physiological response of the body to fear in what is called the "fight or flight" syndrome. However, I know of no scientific studies which show that an adrenalin rush would enable a little ninety-eight pound lady to lift up a *two thousand pound* car. I believe this was an example of the Gift of Faith that produced supernatural strength operating through this little God-fearing, lifetime Methodist lady, during a time of great need for a miracle, to save her husband's life. In this example we see three manifestations of the Holy Spirit occurring: the Gift of Faith, the Spirit of Might, and the Working of Miracles as God intervened into her normal physiology to produce a miracle.

Always remember, when it comes to the Gifts of the Spirit, God gives no preference with respect to persons. Therefore the Holy Spirit can operate the superb Gift of Faith through you, too! Let's move on now to the Gifts of Healings.

Supporting Scriptures:
The Gift of Faith
Please read the scriptures

---

[1] Heb 11:3, Rom 4:17, Col 2:12
[2] Rom 12:3, Eph 2:8 Gal 5:22 Jas 5:15
[3] Rom 4:17, Gen 1:3,6,9,11,14,20,24,26,27, Heb 11:3, Mk 11:22,23
[4] 2 Ki 6:1-7
[5] 1 Sam 17: 1-7
[6] 1 Sa 17: 8-11,16
[7] 1 Sa 17:15,17,18,23,24
[8] 1 Sa 17:26,31

[9] 1 Sa 17:33
[10] 1 Sa 17:34-36
[11] 1 Sa 17:44
[12] 1 Sa 17:45-51
[13] Lk 13:10-17
[14] Lk 11:20
[15] Lk 6:6-10
[16] Mk 2:27
[17] Phil 2:6-8
[18] Acts 3:1-9
[19] Jn 14:14
[20] Mt 17:15-21
[21] Mk 8:22-25
[22] 1 Sa 17:35, 37
[23] 1 Sa 17:47
[24] Gen 17:9,10, Psm 89:34
[25] 1 Cor 11:25, Heb 8:6, 12:24, 13:20,21

CHAPTER NINE

THE GIFTS OF HEALINGS

The Gifts of Healings are particularly valuable to those who are sick, infirmed, or disabled. These Gifts have absolutely nothing to do with the natural healing process, healing through medicine or surgery, or healing through alternative practices using herbs, essential oils, magnetic energy, or other sources to reverse sickness, disease, infirmity, or trauma to the human body. The Gifts of Healings involve the sovereign *supernatural Power* of God, by the Holy Spirit, to heal independently of man or any other natural source. However, man *may be* an *indirect* channel associated with the manifestation of this Gift. Those are the criteria that identify this Gift.

You can be a point of contact for the manifestation of this Gift, if the Holy Spirit wills. Although clearly listed as one of the nine Gifts of the Spirit, examples of the manifestation of *this* Gift appear to be far less prevalent in scripture than the other Gifts.

In the Old Testament

In the Old Testament, the people of God complained and murmured against their leader Moses during their journey through the wilderness. As a result, many were bitten by serpents and died. So the people asked Moses to pray that God would take away the serpents from their midst. God responded by instructing Moses to make a fiery serpent of brass, put it upon a pole, raise it up, and tell the people that if everyone who was bitten by a snake looked upon the brass serpent, they would live. Although Moses and the people each had a role to play indirectly, the healing was supernaturally done by God in a sovereign way.[1]

This example of the Gifts of Healings, represented a *type* and symbol of things to come when the Lord Jesus Christ would be beaten, lifted up on the cross, and we would *behold Him* as the One by whose stripes we are healed.[2]

In the Earthly Life and Ministry of Jesus Christ

In the earthly life and ministry of Jesus we see an excellent example of the Gifts of Healings. After Jesus had chosen His twelve apostles, He and His disciples went down into a flat open space where people from Judaea, Jerusalem, and the seacoast of Tyre and Sidon came to hear Him and to be healed of their diseases. The whole multitude sought and desired to touch Him. Why? Because they were healed by the virtue that flowed out of Him![3] You know what the word "virtue" means? It means supernatural miraculous power! Sick people wanted to touch Him because the *supernatural miraculous power* that flowed out of Him would heal them. Let's get the picture as to what's happening here so we can more clearly understand the Gifts of Healings.

There was a *great* multitude of people in this place with *all kinds* of sicknesses and diseased conditions along with those harassed by demonic spirits. Try to imagine this scene! Visualize a sea of people desperate for help. Some may have been blind, others cripple and unable to walk. All types of people who could have been plagued with leprosy, tumors, palsy, deafness, and all manner of unthinkable diseased conditions came to Jesus to be healed. According to the Word, some were possessed with demons and therefore may have been lunatics, and insane.

This meant that *numerous kinds* of supernatural "gifts" were necessary because *numerous kinds* of supernatural "healings" were required. That's why this particular manifestation of the Holy Spirit is called, in the plural, the "Gifts of Healings." Also, if you read this scriptural passage carefully you will notice that the Word does not mention *any* activity *by Jesus* to heal anyone. Jesus was simply the vessel, or channel, through which the Holy Spirit manifested His supernatural Gifts of Healings so that the *various kinds* of people making up the great multitude could be healed of their *various kinds* of sicknesses and diseases. Got it? Praise God! As a point of contact the Holy Spirit can manifest this Gift through you too, if it is His will.

In the Early Church

In the Early Church, the Apostle Peter encountered a man named Aeneas who was bed ridden for eight years due to palsy. Peter simply told the man, "Jesus Christ maketh thee whole: arise and make thy bed." The man arose immediately! Peter simply spoke the Word and a Gift of Healing manifested in a sovereign way by the Holy Spirit. Scripture gives no other reason for the healing.[4]

We also see something else from the Book of the Acts that's very interesting about Peter and the Gifts of Healings. Scripture states that after a great number of people were added to the church, many of them brought others that were sick and laid them on beds and mats in the streets hoping that at least *the shadow* of Peter passing by would fall on them. It wouldn't make any sense to do that unless *the people had seen others* healed in this manner. In fact, the scripture goes on to say that a multitude came out of cities round about Jerusalem bringing sick folks and those vexed with unclean spirits, and *everyone of them* was healed.[5] This meant that there was virtuous healing power of the Holy Spirit flowing through Peter, as it had flowed through Jesus Christ. The effectiveness of the healing power extended to the length of Peter's shadow. There is no mention of Peter doing *anything whatsoever*, of his own faith or volition, to get the people healed. If people were healed just by Peter's shadow touching them, you'd better believe it was by the majestic Holy Spirit *operating on His own* by manifesting Gifts of Healings; using Peter merely as a point of contact. Awesome! Awesome! Awesome! The Holy Spirit is truly *awesome!*

In the Life and Ministry of the Author

In my life and ministry, the Gifts of Healings have manifested on numerous occasions in public evangelistic services. I did not know about them until testimonies were later given. However, there are times when a Word of Knowledge will reveal a Gift of Healing in operation. Let me explain.

During a ministry meeting with a group of Believers *at a home* in Colorado, a lady who had sustained a serious injury to her ankle was in attendance. Her ankle was severely swollen, she was unable to walk without *extreme* pain, and she had to use crutches. She put her crutches behind the couch and they were out of my sight from where she was sitting during the meeting. I did not see her, know her, see her crutches, or know anything about her condition. But the Holy Spirit gave me a Word of Knowledge that He *was healing* someone with a *severe* ankle injury. Notice: not *wanted to* heal, or was *going to heal*, but, was in *the process of healing*. This was a Word of Knowledge revealing a Gift of Healing in progress.

When this information was told to the people in attendance, the lady with the injury stood up, experienced instant healing, and walked normally without a limp, or pain, or need for crutches. I do not recall praying for her, commanding her ankle to be healed, or laying hands on her *for* healing.

This was a sovereign move of the Holy Spirit releasing a Gift of Healing, independent of man, but *informing us* by a Word of Knowledge *of what He was doing!* My recent understanding is that this lady has never had a problem with that ankle since.

As He wills, the Holy Spirit can have Gifts of Healings flow today as well as in times past. And that's wonderful! Let's now move on and get some insight involving the Gift of the Working of Miracles.

Supporting Scriptures:
The Gifts of Healings
Please read the scriptures

---

[1] Num 21:9

[2] 1 Pe 2:24, Isa 53:5

[3] Lk 6:17-19

[4] Acts 9:32-35

[5] Acts 5: 14-16

CHAPTER TEN

THE WORKING OF MIRACLES

These are among the most dramatic and spectacular operations of the Holy Spirit. The Old Testament is loaded with examples of mighty, phenomenal miracles performed by God alone, as well as those performed by God *through* Old Testament prophets and men of faith. To discuss all of the miracles of the Bible would require another book, so we will limit ourselves to discuss a few examples found in the Old Testament, the earthly life and ministry of Jesus, the Early Church, and from my own life and ministry.

In His earthly life and ministry, Jesus performed a great number of astounding miracles. In the Early Church, God added another class of sovereign miracles called "Special miracles." As we shall see, miracles still occur today.

People attribute many kinds of great *blessings* to miracles. However, the Working of Miracles is far different. The Working of Miracles is a supernatural manifestation of the Holy Spirit whereby God, working *through* man or *independently of* man, intervenes into the components, function, or natural state or existence of something and causes a change to occur. Even from something which does not exist, God can create something which does.

Miracles are always mighty signs and wonders of stupendous proportion. You will know that it is a supernatural work of God because it will transcend any known human or natural capability. Those are the criteria that identify this Gift. Let's survey a few miracles from the Old Testament.

In the Old Testament

In the Old Testament, we find that the Earth was without form, void, and enveloped in darkness. But the Spirit of God, Who is the Holy Spirit, was on the scene. God simply spoke the words, "light be," and by the supernatural Power of the Holy Spirit, "light was."[1] Here we find the unseen God of all gods working with His Son Jesus Christ before He came to earth, and working by the Holy Spirit, supernaturally bring forth light to extinguish the presence of darkness. That's a sovereign God working an awesome miracle.

After Moses died, the Lord appointed Joshua to lead the people of Israel across the Jordan River into the Promised Land God had shown to Moses. Upon entering into the Promised Land, Joshua and his armies went to war against five Amorite kings and their armies. The Lord told Joshua that He would fight his battle. And He did! In fact, He rained down hail and killed more of the enemy than Joshua's men did with the sword! But Joshua wasn't satisfied. He wanted to destroy all of his enemies but he needed more daylight to do so. Now get this! First Joshua prayed to the Lord. Then, *he spoke* to the sun and the moon and told them *to stand still!*[2] By the way, what he did was consistent with the behavior and teaching principles of Jesus.[3]

God listened to Joshua and supernaturally intervened into the laws of physics that govern the functioning of the universe *and stopped* the sun and moon from moving for a whole day. Joshua then continued to complete his battle during daylight. This miracle of God was never done before through man, nor has it been done since.

Another Old Testament miracle of God, indirectly referred to by Jesus and mentioned in other areas of the New Testament, is often discussed in church circles today. It involves a mighty prophet, who is mentioned about a hundred times in the Bible, named Elijah. Elijah's name means *Jehovah is God.* Here's the background.

A king named Ahab did evil in the sight of the Lord more than all of the other previous kings. So God sent His prophet Elijah to tell Ahab that there would be no rain *for years*. That's bad news because if there's no rain, there's no water. No water, no crops. No crops, no food. No food, famine in the land. Here the Holy Spirit, working through Elijah, was manifesting a Word of Wisdom regarding what was going to happen in the future.

After speaking truth to the king in power, Ahab, God told Elijah to go and hide himself by a brook east of Jordan called Cherith; where there would be water, and that he would be fed there by ravens. That's the Word of Wisdom in operation through Elijah providing information *about the future* and giving directions. Things came to pass just as God had shown Elijah, but after awhile the brook dried up because there was no rain.

God then told Elijah to go to a city called Zarephath and dwell there because He had commanded a widow in Zarepath to provide for him. Here's The Word of Wisdom in operation again. Elijah obeyed and sure enough just before entering the gates of Zarepath, he met a widow woman gathering sticks to cook with. He asked her to bring him some water. As she was going to get some water, he asked her to bring him some bread. The woman, probably annoyed at all of these interrupting requests, turned to Elijah and in essence said, "Look, as *your* God lives, I don't have a loaf of bread! All I have is a handful of meal in a jar, and a little oil in a bottle. I'm gathering these two sticks so I can go home and bake it, so me and my son can eat it, *and die!"*

Elijah then, in essence, told the lady, "Don't be afraid, just do what I tell you. Make me a little cake of the meal and oil first, and then make some for your son and yourself." How could Elijah be so sure of himself? Scripture tells us that God had previously spoken to him and told him that the meal would not be depleted, nor would the oil run out, until the day the Lord would send rain again. Elijah told the woman that the Lord had said that! She did as Elijah said to do and every thing worked out exactly as Elijah said it would.[4]

This was the Word of Wisdom being manifested through Elijah again! God told him what to tell the widow woman to do, then He told Elijah that they were going to have provisions in *the future*. The miracle was the continuous supply of food. This is a prime example of God performing a miracle, indirectly involving His servant, to meet the human needs of people in dire circumstances. He hasn't changed, either!

In the Earthly Life and Ministry of Jesus Christ

In the earthly life and ministry of Jesus, we see a number of astounding miracles occurring. We must remember now, that none of the miracles He performed were because of His Godly attributes.[5] He set all of that entirely aside when He came to the Earth. But, He was filled with the Holy Spirit *without measure*, and He was sinless. There was *no limit* as to what the Holy Spirit could do through Him.

Just as the miracle God performed through Elijah was to meet the personal needs of a widow woman, the *first* miracle God performed through Jesus was to meet the personal needs of a bride groom who would have been embarrassed had the wine at his wedding feast run out. By the Holy Spirit, through Jesus, God intervened into the *laws of chemistry* and created wine from a liquid that was water.[6] Wow! You see, God cares about the practical needs of people. Here, God had the Holy Spirit glorify Jesus *even before* He went to the cross. Now He wants the Holy Spirit to glorify Jesus *through you and me!*

Another astounding miracle of God occurred when Jesus walked on water going to the aid of His disciples caught in a storm on the sea. Here we see the intervention of God by the Holy Spirit into the *laws of physics* where the force of gravity is defied as Jesus literally walks on the water.[7] Once again, we see God performing a miracle to *get help to people* in a dire need and circumstance.

The last miracle we will discuss in the earthly life and ministry of Jesus is truly magnificent. It is a miracle which characterizes the whole essence of Jesus. Love!

Right after Jesus was betrayed by Judas, a band of men armed with swords and staves came forth to take Him by force so they could proceed to have Him crucified. But Peter drew *his* sword and while obviously going for the head of a man named Malchus, a servant of the high priest, he missed the head but cut off the man's ear. Without praying, without resisting, without talking, Jesus simply miraculously attached the ear back onto the man's head.[8] Here we see God, through Jesus Christ, supernaturally intervening into the *laws of nature* that govern anatomy, biophysics, and biochemistry. This is a healing miracle of the highest order, so let's look at what's behind it.

The role of Jesus, during His earthly life and ministry, was to reveal the nature and character of God the Father, demonstrate the kingdom of God, and destroy the works of the devil. But God *is* love, so the primary characteristic of His Son is love.[9] In this miracle, we see the manifestation of the love of God, and the demonstrated difference as to how people of the Kingdom of God respond to hostility, compared to responses given by people indoctrinated to the kingdom of *this* world's system.

Imagine for a moment, that for no good reason at all, you have enemies trying to capture you to put you to death even though you are harmless and innocent. Imagine one of your closest friends trying to protect you with a sword and managing to at least cut off the ear of one of your enemies. Can you imagine telling your friend to put away the sword, and then perform a miracle by reattaching the completely severed ear back onto the head of one of the men trying to capture you, and cause you to be put to death? That is exactly what Jesus did.

If you read the Gospels very carefully, you will find that the main emotion driving Jesus to heal was compassion. To me, love and compassion seem to be a major factor in the manifestation of the Gifts of Divine Power and Ability manifested by the Holy Spirit. By working *this* miracle through the Holy Spirit, Jesus was demonstrating the love and compassion of God even towards His enemies! The actions of His enemies, and the response of Peter to those actions, are typical behavioral principles associated with the kingdom of *this* world and *this* world's systems. **Violence using the Name of Christ, whether political, religious, *or for any other cause, is utterly* demonic and has absolutely no sanction for those who belong to the Lord Jesus Christ.** Jesus demonstrated that the Kingdom of God is based upon entirely different principles, and those principles were confirmed by this healing miracle based on love.

In the Early Church

The miracles performed by saints in the Early Church are not as numerous as those seen in the Old Testament and in the earthly life and ministry of Jesus. However the ones that did occur are very significant. Given the extensive occult and paranormal activities evident throughout the world today, it is timely to review a miracle of judgment God performed through the Apostle Paul. Activities of witchcraft, sorcery, the occult, the paranormal, and idolatry are activities which are under satanic control or influence. These are instruments some people *purposefully* use today to thwart the will and purposes of God. God's primary will is eternal life for all through Christ Jesus, and He cuts no slack for people who willfully and knowingly try to deceive and prevent others from receiving this eternal salvation. Let's look at scriptural proof that this is true, and see the Working of a Miracle that was involved.

The Holy Spirit sent the Apostle Paul, who at that time was called Saul, and the Apostle Barnabas on a mission to preach the Word about eternal salvation through Jesus Christ, and about the Kingdom of God. During the journey, they encountered a false prophet named Bar-Jesus, also called Elymas.

Elymas was closely associated with a governmental official in the area named Sergius Paulus, who the Bible says was an intelligent and sensible man with sound understanding. Paulus sent for Paul and Barnabus because he wanted to hear the Word of God concerning salvation through Jesus Christ and hear about the Kingdom of God. But this is what was going on!

Elymas was a sorcerer, a wizard, who deliberately opposed Paul and did every thing he knew to do *to prevent* the proconsul Paulus from receiving salvation through Jesus Christ. Satan uses evil spirits and his *human* satanic operatives of magic, witchcraft, sorcery and so forth, to deliberately deceive, confuse, divert and prevent people from receiving true knowledge that would lead them to eternal salvation through the Lord Jesus Christ.[10] Now watch the Holy Spirit in awesome action *through* Paul!

Paul, being filled and *controlled by* the Holy Spirit, fixed his eyes on this guy. Then Paul by the Spirit said to Elymas, "You master in *every form of deception* and recklessness, unscrupulousness and *wickedness*, you *son of the devil*, you *enemy* of everything that is upright and good, will you never stop perverting and make crooked the straight paths of the Lord *and plotting against* His *saving purposes?"* Wow! I mean these are some extremely serious words *coming from the Holy Spirit through Paul.* Now, following these words spoken, the Working of Miracles through Paul by the Holy Spirit occurred.

Paul tells Elymas, "Lo, the Hand of the Lord is upon *you*, and you shall *be blind*, so blind that you will be unable *to see the sun* for a time." Then the scripture says, "*Instantly* there fell a mist and darkness upon him and he went groping around seeking someone to lead him by the hand."[11]

There's a clear lesson here! Never hinder *anyone* from receiving salvation through Jesus Christ and knowledge about the Kingdom of God. If you see somebody deliberately, consciously, and knowingly, try to hinder another in this process, warn that person! Show him *this* passage of scripture! It's Acts, chapter thirteen, verses four through twelve. There were other noteworthy miracles performed through men by the Holy Spirit in the Early Church, but the Holy Spirit wanted *this one* thoroughly emphasized. It's a *huge mistake* for anyone to interfere with God's effort to save someone through Christ Jesus!

Special Miracles

Scripture gives another classification of miracles done through man by the Holy Spirit called *special miracles*. In the Book of the Acts, scripture tells us that God, by the Holy Spirit, wrought *special miracles* through the hands of the Apostle Paul. Here's how it worked.

At certain times or on certain occasions, the miracle working Power of the Holy Spirit was *so intense* flowing through Paul that it even remained in the clothes he was wearing or carrying on his body. *During those times* if handkerchiefs or aprons which he wore were taken from his body and carried to the sick, the residual supernatural miracle working Power of the Holy Spirit in them would cause people needing healing to be healed, and drove out demons from people who were demon possessed.[12] This type of astounding miracle can be understood if we realize that some spiritual principles are mirrored by natural physical principles which can be understood. Let's explain this by using a common medical example.

Suppose a person with a very powerful respiratory infection sneezes on a door handle. Infectious live bacteria will then be deposited upon the door handle. In medical terms an object harboring live bacteria or other pathogens is called a "formite." It acts as a point of contact *from which* the live bacteria can be transferred to any person or thing that touches it.

If another person now touches the door handle with

their hand and puts that same hand into the mouth or nose, he or she now receives the same live bacteria from the door handle *that was in* the original person, and the bacteria will produce the same effects. Now let's compare and notice the similarity of this natural principle to the spiritual principle involved in "special miracles."

The anointing of the Holy Spirit on the Apostle Paul not only meant that he was saturated with the Power of God, but that his clothes were too; since they touched and were in constant contact with him. His clothes then, harbored the anointing Power of God and were a point of contact *from which* that anointing Power could be transferred to anyone who touched them.

Therefore, anyone who touched his clothes or handkerchiefs would come into contact with the same anointing Power that flowed through Paul. That anointing Power would produce the same effects on a person touching the handkerchief, as it would if the person was being touched by Paul himself. **Just as the door handle acted as a point of contact for a person to receive the bacteria and its effects to cause sickness, the handkerchief acts as a point of contract for a person to receive the anointing Power of the Holy Spirit and its effects to cause healing.** Now, as we're going to see next, this phenomenal type of miracle done by the Holy Spirit through Paul in the Early Church, *is still being done today!*

In the Life and Ministry of the Author

Here's an example of *special miracles* operating through my life and ministry. It's a little lengthy, but well worth reading because it gives great insight into the heart of

God to bless the people He has created.

It was in the Springtime again when the Spirit of God spoke to me and told me to hold public meetings in the month of November in Denver, Colorado. I was even given specific dates. My immediate response was, "Lord, come on now, You know I can't stand cold weather, and it's cold in Denver at that time of the year. Besides Lord, if this is *really* You, those dates will fall on a Thursday, Friday, and Saturday!" I said that because I wanted to test the spirit to see if it was of God, or not. I also knew that the Holy Spirit knew that I always tried to avoid holding public services on Sundays, or Wednesday nights. This way I would avoid interfering with local church services which usually occur during those times. So I went to the calendar to check out the dates. Sure enough, the dates fell on a Thursday, Friday, and Saturday. I was then confident that it was the Holy Spirit that I heard, and that *He was sending me* to Denver for special reasons. After months of preparation through prayer and study of the Word, I left for Denver to conduct services that were scheduled for late November, but ending before Thanksgiving.

It is normally *very* cold, and sometimes it even snows in Denver during that time of the year. I was dressed accordingly but on this particular occasion, a "freak" weather pattern occurred in the Denver area and the temperature remained in the sixties from the day I arrived, until the day I left! Then the temperature plummeted again. I can't prove it, but to this day I believe God remembered my attitude towards cold weather and decided to bless me for being obedient to Him by going. He is thoughtful of you, when you are thoughtful and obedient to Him. Now, we'll see His love poured out to someone who needed His miracle-working help desperately.

Remembering that God did special miracles through the hands of Paul, each night following the ministry of the Holy Spirit, I would lay my hands upon handkerchiefs to be given to people who were unable to attend the services. During one of those services, a handkerchief was taken to a lady who was unable to attend. I never knew if the Holy Spirit had performed a *special miracle*, similar to those He did through the Apostle Paul, in any of our meetings until I received the following letter. Read it carefully!

The Letter About a Special Miracle

Dear Dr. Givens:

In November 1985 I was in a car accident and was injured. I have gone through the many doctors, physical therapists, medications and all the pain and psychological problems that go along with car accidents. I was stopped at a red light and rear-ended by a dump truck.

Well – the whole body got progressively worse. There were times I could not turn over in bed. My spine was "a mess". In April of this year – on April 4, 1987, I could not stand erect – but like an upside down "L," and the pain in my back radiated down my right leg – it was numb, with electricity-like pain, excruciating pain – crutches were the only way I could walk.

A friend of mine had told me about your services and I had planned to attend that evening at the East Denver, Colorado YMCA. When the time had arrived I was in such pain and absolutely could not walk. I called my friend and told her my situation. She had told me that you were anointing handkerchiefs – Well, I didn't have one and she told me that she had many – I then asked her if she would get one anointed for me, and she

did – with my name written on it. My husband went to her house the next day and brought it back to me. Dr. Givens, I had never done this before but I lay there in the bed and I placed the handkerchief on my leg, my back, and I just held it and prayed and the pain started leaving, and leaving. Praise the Lord I can walk without crutches.

In April I had tests and CAT scans. There were bulges between the discs in my spine. In June I had very sophisticated imaging – no bulges between the discs.

I thank the Lord and you for my healing.

Sincerely, Mrs. CT,
Denver, Colorado

This lady gave an astounding testimony about this miracle at our services in Denver a year later. Then she walked smartly up and down the isle to show the magnificent miracle Jesus Christ had done for her. The Holy Spirit still works *special miracles* today. And by the way, just don't forget that the Lord is no respecter of persons.[13]

How Multiple Gifts Coordinate for Miracles

In 1988 my wife and I were graced to hold five days of ministry services at a church in Atlanta, Georgia. The manifestation of the Gifts of the Spirit *to glorify the Lord Jesus Christ* were so profound that all of us; the Pastor, the congregation, my wife and I, were absolutely astounded. The Holy Spirit revealed and successfully ministered to people with conditions ranging from a man desiring a brown suit, a spirit of fear that was harassing a police officer, children afflicted with spontaneous nose bleeds, a woman with a cyst on her left ovary, to a woman with a tumor in her left breast.

The Lord clearly used the services to *reveal* the Lord Jesus Christ, to *demonstrate* the Kingdom of God and *the ministry of the Holy Spirit* in a profound way, and to show how people are drawn to Him because of His glory and saving grace.

I perceive that the Holy Spirit wants me to share with you two things about the manifestation of His Gifts which are just as applicable today as they were in those services, namely: how specific He is in manifesting His Gifts, and how His Gifts often coordinate for spectacular results.

The Holy Spirit's way of being specific rules out fraud and abuse. We are living at a time where Satan will use con artists to deceive even the elect.[A] The Holy Spirit is extremely specific in what He reveals through a Word of Knowledge. For example: He won't just say someone has a pain in the head! *Anyone* can tell a congregation, "Someone has a pain in the head." And the larger the congregation is, the more likely there *would* be *someone*, or even many, with pain in the head. Plus, that information just may not be coming from the Holy Spirit, but from someone acting *as though* it is. That's *deception*, and it does occur! The Holy Spirit is *so specific* that He wills not only to reveal that someone has pain in the head, but He usually describes the location as to where it is in the head, the type of pain it is, and *how the pain is manifested.*

Here's an example of what I mean. To say that someone has pain in the head *is one thing*. But to say that someone has pain that starts on the left side of the head, near the superior attachment of the temporal muscle to

---

[A] **Read How to Avoid Spiritual Deception very carefully**

the occipital bone, that is sharp when you bend over, then radiates like electricity to the middle of the back of the neck on the same side when you stand up, *is quite another! That* can't be faked. And the person for whom that information is revealed knows exactly that it applies to him or her, and knows assuredly that it has come from the Spirit of God. The Holy Spirit is just that specific.

Now, from the ministry services we conducted in Atlanta, let me give you a real life example of this type specificity, and at the same time, illustrate how the Gifts of the Spirit can coordinate one with another.[B]

The Holy Spirit revealed *to my wife* that there was a woman in the congregation that had pain in her *left hip*, and that she had difficulty *standing up when sitting*, and *sitting down* when she was *standing up*. Then the Holy Spirit revealed *to me* that the left leg was *shorter than the right leg*. That's six *specific pieces of information* about that one over all condition which involved a woman, pain, the left hip, difficulty standing up when sitting, difficulty sitting down when standing, and a left leg shorter than the right leg. Then the lady responding volunteered information that her doctors diagnosed problems related to the vertebrae of her back. Could there be any doubt in this woman's mind that the Holy Spirit was speaking directly to her? Since she was the only one in that large congregation who came forward to be ministered to, could there be any doubt in *anyone else's mind* that this indeed was revealed from the Holy Spirit? If there was, you'll see in a moment how that doubt had to be removed!

Here we see a Word of Knowledge given to my wife, and a Word of Knowledge given to me, about the same

---

[B] **These events were edited from a taped recording of the actual Services**

conditions affecting the same person. Then, the Holy Spirit placed the Gift of Faith into my spirit that He was going to perform a miracle by growing out the left leg which was over an inch shorter than the right leg. *Before* it happened, I told the congregation that the miracle was going to occur. After speaking and commanding the leg to grow out in the Name of Jesus, God *quickly* performed the miracle. All of the lady's problems associated with her back and hip were solved, and her short leg was made whole like the other. If there was any doubt, from anyone, about the reality of the Holy Spirit and His ability, I guarantee that that doubt left! This was a mighty miracle!

Here then, we see a practical real life example as to how the Holy Spirit *identified* a problem with one Gift; The Word of Knowledge. Then He *brought special faith* against that problem with another Gift; The Gift of Faith, and then with a *supernatural miraculous manifestation of power* eliminated the problem with a third Gift; The Working of Miracles. This was *all done by the Holy Spirit* with three Gifts working together in coordinated harmony *to glorify* the Lord Jesus Christ. Awesome. The Holy Spirit is absolutely *awesome!*

Supporting Scriptures:
The Working of Miracles
Please read the scriptures

---

[1] Gen 1:1-3
[2] Josh 10:11-14
[3] Mk 4:39, 11:23
[4] 1 Kin 17:1-16
[5] Phil 2:6-8

[6] Jn 2:1-11

[7] Mk 6:47, 48,49

[8] Lk 22:50-51

[9] Jn 1:18, 14:7, Jn 10:30, Jn 5:17, 1 Jn 3:8, 1 Jn 4:8, 16, Jn 3:16, 2Cor 13:11,

[10] Acts 8:9-11, Ex 7:11, Dan 2:2, Rev 21:8

[11] Acts 13: 4-12

[12] Acts 19:11,12

[13] Acts 10:34

THE GIFTS OF DIVINE VOCAL COMMUNICATION

The third and final group of the Gifts of the Holy Spirit that we will discuss is The Gifts of Divine Vocal Communication. These supernatural Gifts are The Gift of Tongues, The Interpretation of Tongues, and The Gift of Prophecy. These Gifts can be misunderstood, used in error, misused, and even abused. But with the help of the Holy Spirit, let's believe God to shed truth and light to us about these Gifts.

Prior to discussing these Gifts, it is essential to have some additional understanding of an activity exercised by many Believers called *speaking in tongues*. I am fully aware that to some, speaking in tongues is thought to be absolute *nonsense*. Scripturally, speaking in tongues has broad application to many spiritual activities and is an essential component of several of the Gifts of Divine Vocal Communication.

Speaking in tongues did not occur in the Old Testament, nor during the time period of the earthly life and ministry of Jesus Christ. Speaking in tongues is strictly a New Testament church activity manifested by the Holy Spirit that did not occur until what is called the Day of Pentecost. Speaking in tongues will continue until the end of this time period called the Dispensation of Grace. Tongues occur at *different times* and for *different purposes*. [A]

[A] **Review "Essential Steps to Take: The Value of Tongues. Other Uses for Tongues" Pages 218, 219.**

Speaking in tongues has absolutely nothing whatsoever to do with receiving eternal salvation through Christ Jesus. Those who wrongfully believe that it does are in gross error and totally without scriptural support for such belief. But as we shall see later, speaking in tongues is scriptural proof of being baptised with the Holy Spirit.

Chapter Eleven

THE GIFT OF TONGUES

The Gift of Tongues, also referred to as "tongues," is a supernatural gift given by the Holy Spirit that has nothing to do with a person's linguistic ability. Just as *we have* the ability to use our tongues to speak different languages, the Holy Spirit has the ability to use our tongues to speak utterances and different languages. Some of the languages and utterances are known to us, some are known to others but not to us, and some are known only to God.

However, the Gift of Tongues is a supernatural utterance given by the Holy Spirit in a language that *the speaker* does not know. Those are the criteria that identify this Gift. The language may be one spoken and understood by mankind, or it may not be understood by mankind. This is what the Apostle Paul meant when he said that he spoke with the tongues of men *and angels*.[1] There are thousands of languages and dialects spoken throughout the Earth today. The Holy Spirit, through supernatural means, can cause any language or dialect to be spoken through a person as He wills, or He can manifest a language or dialect *unknown to anyone* but God.

The Interpretation of Tongues

The Interpretation of Tongues involves *the person who hears* and the individual *speaking* through the Gift of Tongues. If the tongues spoken were in a language the hearer understood, he or she can give a natural interpretation of what was spoken. If a hearer does not understand the language spoken, the Holy Spirit can supernaturally move upon him, or another hearer, to give understanding. The person who receives the understanding from the Holy Spirit can then translate it to others so that they too may understand what the message was that the Spirit gave. These criteria identify this Gift. On occasion more than one person will receive the exact same interpretation of what the Holy Spirit said through the speaker.

There are times when the Holy Spirit will choose to give a message in tongues that the speaker does not understand, and then supernaturally move upon *that same* speaker and give understanding. That speaker can then communicate the message received from the Holy Spirit to others. Although the Gift of Tongues and the Interpretation of Tongues *can* occur on a private individual basis, they mostly occur during church services or meetings. Believers are instructed to pray for the ability to interpret Tongues given by the Holy Spirit.[2]

Supporting Scriptures:
The Gift of Tongues,
The Interpretation of Tongues
Please read the scriptures

---

[1] 1 Cor 13:1

[2] 1 Cor 14:13

Chapter Twelve

THE GIFT OF PROPHECY

The Gift of Prophecy is the final Gift of the Holy Spirit that we shall discuss. The reason I saved it for last is because the Apostle Paul infers that it is *the best* of all of the Gifts of the Spirit. There *are* true Prophets in the Body of Christ today, and we are told in Scripture to not despise prophesying.[1]

The Gift of Prophecy is supernatural speech inspired by God spoken through a Believer in a *known tongue.* In other words, the person being used by the Holy Spirit speaks in a language he or she understands to a person or people who also understand the same language. Those are the criteria that identify this Gift.

The person speaks under the influence of the Holy Spirit, not from something he thinks up. The Holy Spirit causes the person speaking to use his own natural language. Therefore, the person speaking as well as all present, know exactly what the Spirit of God is saying. The Gift of Prophecy will often incorporate the Word of Knowledge, or the Word of Wisdom.

The Gift of Prophecy falls into two distinct categories. One category relates strictly to the Church and its individual Believers. This is called "simple prophecy." This type of prophecy is scripture based and always gives edification, exhortation, and comfort. It gives strength, encouragement, and builds up the body of Believers. It *is not* predictive.

The other type of prophecy flows by the Holy Spirit through a person who stands in what is called the Office of the Prophet, as a prophet. Prophecy of this type *is* predictive. From the Old Testament, we can see an example of both types of prophecy.

In the Old Testament

There was a king in Israel named Asa who ruled at a time when there was near complete chaos in the society. Nations were fighting against nations, cities against cities, and people were vexed with all kinds of adversities at a time when Israel had no teaching priests. Nonetheless, Asa did what was right and good in the sight of the Lord. He tore down things related to idol worship and built up the things that pertained to the Lord. Whenever he and his allies were in danger, or went to war, he sought the Lord with all of his heart and depended *only* upon the Lord for help and victory.

The Lord was very pleased with him. As a result, the Spirit of God came upon a young man and gave him great words of edification, exhortation, and comfort for King Asa. This was simple prophecy. The young man's name was Azariah, whose father was a prophet named Oded.

Later on in life, the King's behavior changed. He no longer sought the Lord *for anything*. The time came when he was faced with war again. This time, instead of seeking counsel and help from the Lord, on his own initiative he sought the help of the King of Syria; who was weaker in military strength than he was. He even went so far as to take silver and gold *from the house of the Lord* to pay the King of Syria to be on his side!

Therefore, God now sent the prophet Hanani to King Asa. By the Spirit, the prophet reminded him of so many great things that were done for him when he relied upon the Lord. The prophet told him that *now* he had done foolishly by no longer relying upon the Lord. Furthermore, he was told that in the future he would even have wars.

Now get this! King Asa knew this man was a prophet of God! Yet instead of turning back to the Lord, he became furious at the prophet for the words he heard coming *from* the Lord *through* the prophet, and actually had the prophet thrown into prison. A little while later, the King's feet became diseased. The physicians he sought could not help him and he refused to turn back to the Lord. The wars did come upon him, and he died from his diseased feet.[2]

In this Old Testament passage of scripture we see the two types of prophecy given by the Spirit of God. Azariah gave the King simple prophecy that gave edification, exhortation, and comfort. But Hanani, who stood in the Office of the Prophet, gave the King strong words *that predicted the future*. Things came to pass just as the prophet had predicted.

In the Earthly Life and Ministry of Jesus Christ

In the earthly life and ministry of Jesus, we see the greatest of all Prophets, Jesus Himself. Through the Spirit of prophecy He predicted His own death, burial, and resurrection which came to pass exactly as He said it would. In addition, He fulfilled all of the Old Testament prophecies about Him concerning His earthly life and ministry.[3]

In the Early Church

In the Early Church, we find from The Book of The Revelation, numerous prophecies given by Jesus to the Apostle John regarding things that were to come pertaining to Believers, non-believers, Satan and those under his authority.

A Word of Caution

A word of caution is warranted regarding people who continually seek "a prophet" in order to receive "a word from the Lord." The Lord is very capable of giving you "a word" Himself. The more sure word of prophecy is scripture itself.

Predictive prophecy today is misused and abused more than any other spiritual gift. Anytime you receive "a word" from any source, make absolutely sure it lines up with scripture and is in line with sound Biblical doctrine. It should edify, exhort, comfort, and give you peace in your spirit. Make sure *you are not obligated or required to make any commitment of any kind* to the person giving you "the word of personal prophecy," or others associated with that person.

Supporting Scriptures:
The Gift of Prophecy
Please read the scriptures

---

[1] 1 Cor 14:1, 5, 39, 1 Thess 4:20

[2] 1 Kin 15:11, 2Chr 16:1-4, 7-10, 12, 13

[3] Mt 20:17-19 Mt 5:17 Jn 4:19-26, Gen 3:15
Is 40:1-5,9-11, Is 35:4-6 Duet 18:15-18 Zec 9:9,
Is 9:6,7

CHAPTER THIRTEEN

SUPERNATURAL VOICES

Since the Divine Vocal Communication Gifts and other manifestations of the Holy Spirit can involve hearing what is spoken from God, this is an excellent time to comment on *hearing voices*.

Trying to *hear voices*, hoping that it's God's voice, can be extremely dangerous. However, there are several ways God *can* speak to a person through words. He can speak words directly to you by the Holy Spirit, to you by a Gift of the Holy Spirit given through another person, or by an angel. There are voices in the spirit realm that we can sometimes hear in this natural, physical realm. We must be able to tell the difference between the voice of God, and the voice of an evil spirit speaking by the authority of Satan.

Whenever anyone says "God spoke to me," or "Jesus said to me," he or she really means that the Holy Spirit spoke to him or her. God and Jesus *do not* speak to us directly. They speak through the Holy Spirit. The Holy Spirit speaks to us what He hears from either Jesus, or the Father. I cannot tell you how He speaks to others, and I don't know how He will speak to you. But I do know how He speaks to me. I will share with you my personal and ministerial experiences of over twenty-five years concerning hearing different types of spiritual voices. As previously stated, the voice of God comes directly from the Holy Spirit, or through people speaking by the Holy Spirit. Voices from evil spirits, and voices through people who are under the control or possession of evil spirits, are *deceptive* and *dangerous*.

Undoubtedly, you've heard people who have committed extremely horrible crimes that said, "I heard a voice tell me to do it," or, "God told me to do it!" Many of them *think* they are telling the truth. But they are totally deceived! They were under the influence of an evil spirit, or they were actually possessed by an evil spirit and could hear *instructions* given to them by that evil spirit.

This is what I have observed: whenever the Spirit of God speaks to me, ninety per cent of the time it is directly according to scripture, or it is scripturally related. The very *first time* I heard the voice of God occurred when I became very serious about the things of God. The voice said, "So shall my Word be that goeth forth out of my mouth, it shall not return unto me void but accomplish that which I please and it shall prosper in the thing whereto I sent it." I had never heard those words before in my life. I didn't know they existed. But when I checked them out, I discovered they were Biblical scriptures from the fifty-fifth chapter of Isaiah. God was telling me, *by speaking to me through scripture itself*, about the reliability and performance of His Word. On another occasion, I heard the voice of God tell me, "All who call upon the Name of the Lord shall be saved." Again, *scripture* was spoken to me.

On one occasion I heard the Spirit of God say to me, "In Him dwelleth all of the fullness of the Godhead bodily; and ye are complete in Him." The Lord was telling me by the Spirit *who* is in Christ, and what *I am* in Him: complete! Once again, scripture was spoken to me. By the way, let me share something about this scripture that I think you'll find fantastic. It's also a revelation that provides tremendous insight.

We *receive* Jesus by our faith. But being in Christ *is not* something we receive as a function of *our* faith. We are *placed* into *Christ* by the Holy Spirit, and it is the Holy Spirit who also places Christ in us. Imagine a hand and glove where *you* are the hand, *He* is the glove, and the hand *is enveloped* in the glove. Being in Christ means that we are enveloped by Him. That is how we become one; Him being the Head, and we being His Body.[A] Now back to supernatural voices.

Most of the time, whenever I hear the voice of God it is usually very gentle. But it *can* be moderately strong. It is normally heard from within; kind of like what you hear when you read a book to yourself with your mouth closed. But *on rare occasions* it seems to almost be heard externally, as though someone else is speaking. If the voice heard *is not direct* scripture, but is *scripturally related*, it always gives great insight and is for good. Next, let me share with you several occasions where the voice I heard was from an evil spirit that had evil intentions.

While ministering in New York the Holy Spirit revealed to me through a Word of Knowledge that there was a person in the congregation that had an infection involving the first joint and fingernail bed of the middle finger of the right hand. Pretty specific! He, the Holy Spirit, wanted to heal it. After I revealed this to the congregation, a middle aged woman came forth and stretched out her hand. I saw the most gross, and wicked looking fungal infection that I had ever seen professionally or otherwise. I mean, it was nasty! Now get this! While looking at this horrible sight I heard a strong voice say to me, "Kiss it!" My first reaction

---

[A] **Use a good biblical concordance and do a comprehensive word study of Col 2:9, 10; especially as it relates to "in Him." What you will discover will bless you beyond measure!**

was a sarcastic, "I don't *think* so." But check this! For a split moment I thought to myself, "Jesus did some weird things when healing people. He spat in mud and put it on a blind man's eyes!"

Look what Satan was doing! He was putting scripture into my mind to pervert my response to a demonic condition, and at the same time tried to put me into a guilt trip of obedience. In other words, he seemed to be saying, "Jesus did something that didn't seem natural, why don't *you* do something like that, too!" With that thought, the Voice of God *instantly* spoke to me and said, "You're not given a spirit of fear, but of power, love, and a sound mind!" *Then He explained it just like this:* "power, because you have all power through my Name and the Holy Spirit. Love, because love conquers all. A sound mind, because your mind is renewed by the Word of God, *and as a professional man you're not stupid enough to kiss that thing!"* This sequence of voices all happened at a rapid speed of thought.

Needless to say, with common sense and the words God gave to me, I did not respond with a ridiculous kiss to her finger. Instead of kissing that demonic condition, I cursed it in the Name of Jesus Christ, commanded it to dry up, die, and to go from that woman's finger. But notice, once again the Holy Spirit's *initial* words to me were given *in scripture*.

The experience you have just read about happened during a ministry service. Now I'm going to share with you a personal situation that happened to me when I heard a voice, and got confused about it. This happened *before* I went into "the Ministry." While being sick one Saturday evening, I decided to commune with the Lord and tell Him that, "By His stripes I am healed." That's a potent healing scripture. After doing this for about an hour I began to feel better and started to doze off to sleep still muttering, "Jesus, by Your stripes I am healed." All of a sudden I heard this mean, loud voice on the inside say, "Stop it!" That got my attention *very* quickly. The thought came to my mind that perhaps Jesus felt that I was just mouthing off, not paying attention, and falling half way to sleep. I sure didn't want to get the Lord ticked off at me, so I stopped![B]

After church the following day, I related what had happened to me to my Pastor. He smiled and said, "That wasn't the voice of God your heard. The Lord would *never* under any circumstance tell you *to stop speaking scriptures*." He was right.

Okay. Hearing and obeying a voice can end up being a major blessing or a major disaster; depending on whether it's the voice of God, or the voice of an evil spirit. You have to determine if the words you hear are of God or not. In my experience, it all depends upon whether the words I hear are scriptural or scripturally based. Are the words of benefit to me or others, or are they words of condemnation, scorn or ones that would lead to unwise behavior? Is the tone mean and frightful, or gentle and kind? One set of words demonstrate love, the other does not. God is love.

In the final analysis not a person, nor tapes, nor books, can tell you how to hear the voice of God. If you belong to Jesus Christ, you already have the greatest Teacher there is who can help you. That Teacher is the Holy Spirit. Pray, and ask Him to teach you to hear the voice of God.

[B] **God is pure love and does not get "ticked off". However, He will deal harshly with the wicked and those who are evil, in the future. See Rev. 21:8**

CHAPTER FOURTEEN

HOW TO IDENTIFY SUPERNATURAL DECEPTION

Supernatural manifestations, whether they are miracles, healings, prophetic utterances, or of some other type, are derived from *one* of two sources: Godly power, or evil power. Regardless of how wonderful the manifestation *may appear* to be, *its source* can still be evil and have a devastating effect *on you.* The Holy Spirit wants us to be able to *tell the difference* as to whether the manifestation is from the Spirit of God or from a source that is not of God. Supernatural deception can be identified *for us* by the Holy Spirit and shown to us *for recognition* from the Word of God. *This is critical information to know.*

Spiritual and Supernatural Deception

Supernatural deception is *spiritual deception*, but not all spiritual deception is *supernatural.* For example, a "fortune teller" operating under the influence of a familiar spirit may describe to you a person you met in the past, and tell you "she sees" that you should marry that person. That is deceptive *supernatural* information coming to her from a source of evil power. Then he or she may pretend that the information revealed came directly from God. *That information is not supernatural.* It is *spiritual deception* about God that is an outright lie.

Supernatural deception is not new. It was even

encountered by Moses.[1] Operatives who use spiritual deception, regardless of the methods they practice; whether supernatural or not, are despised by God and will receive His most harsh, ultimate penalty.[2] The reason it is so extremely important for us to recognize and understand spiritual deception today is that we are living in exceedingly perilous times where "End Time" prophetic Biblical scripture *and* world history have come together. Various types of evil spiritual manifestations and operatives are active today and will intensify their activities in the future.[3] They will eventually manifest such great deceptive supernatural manifestations, that great multitudes throughout nations will be deceived to their own tragic detriment. *But not you! Not after reading this book!*

According to scripture there are false apostles, workers, and teachers operating *even in some churches*, today! This is why we *must know* and *be adamant* about sound scriptural doctrine based on the Word of God and rely upon the Holy Spirit to reveal the truth to us. This coverage is lengthy, *but it is extremely important to know.* Study the supporting scriptures provided and stay focused to see some spiritual truths that you may not have fully understood, or may not have been taught.

What Deception Is

Before discussing supernatural deception let's get an understanding as to what *deception* is, and discover some of the various types of deception. Spiritual deception is so important to understand because it is the major tool Satan uses in his effort to steal, kill, and destroy people that God has created.

Deception is an intentional act to mislead someone

from the truth. Deception is illusionary, it can be ambiguous, and it is fraud. It is a hoax, it is a sham, it is tricky, it is treacherous, and it is *evil.* It leads to that which is false, and concludes in being that which is a lie. The father and originator of lies is Satan.[4]

There are two categories of deception: Deception using natural means, and deception using spiritual means. Deception using spiritual means can be supernatural, or *non* supernatural. The resulting intent is nevertheless the same since both types are sources for destruction and harm. Let's take a look at this a little further.

Natural Deception

Suppose a General at war *must* capture and occupy a particular area that is very heavily defended with numerous enemy troops. He realizes that he cannot be successful because of the concentration and number of enemy troops protecting that area. So he sets a plan in motion designed to cause the opposing generals to withdraw their troops to another location.

Our General has absolutely no intention of altering his original battle plan. But he writes up a new order of battle detailing how he is actually going to attack a *different* important location a hundred miles away, two days later.

The General then sees to it that the bogus plan "accidently" falls into the hands of a known enemy spy. In a short period of time the bogus plan ends up in the hands of enemy generals who are convinced that the plan's battle orders to attack *at a different location* is authentic, can be done, is brilliant, and that our General's troops in *the current* location are just there as a decoy to cover his *real intention.* So new orders are given by the enemy generals to immediately withdraw all troops and equipment *from* their present location, and deploy *to* the new location where the enemy believes the real attack will occur two days later. This is exactly what our General wanted the enemy to do.

Two days later our General executes his original attack plan, captures and occupies his target area, and there is nothing the enemy a hundred miles away can do about it. They were deceived and swallowed the lie. This is an example of pure *natural deception*. It is used commonly in military situations today, and it has been used throughout history. In the Old Testament we see a wonderful example of the Holy Spirit revealing a king's military plans to a prophet of God who then told them to the King of Israel during a time of war.[5] The Holy Spirit can expose *anything*.

The Holy Spirit and Spiritual Deception

People can be deceived by natural and spiritual means. The Holy Spirit, however, can expose and reveal both. Spiritual deception, whether occurring as false *supernatural* lying signs and wonders, or distortion and false manipulation of the Word of God, is so dangerous to our salvation through Christ Jesus that the Holy Spirit will expose it to us. Based upon scriptural facts, here's how I believe the Holy Spirit's process to expose deception works.

The Word of God *is true* and the Word of God *is spirit*. The Holy Spirit knows the true *Word* of God, He performs the true Works of God, and *He is the Power* of God. As the Spirit of Truth, He knows if the words He hears *are not* of God, but are false and deceptive words from a source that is evil. He knows if *the works* or manifestations He sees *are not His* and therefore are false and deceptive works from a source that is evil. And, He knows when the supernatural power being demonstrated *is not His!* The Holy

Spirit then exposes and reveals this information to us. **With the Holy Spirit and insight from the Word of God we have the means to identify *spiritual deception* regardless of the form that it takes.**

The Origin and Progression of Deception

To understand the spiritual reality of *the present*, we must know the *scriptural* history of *spiritual events* that have occurred in the past. This will help us to see the origin of deception and enable us to clearly *understand* and *recognize* the difference between supernatural manifestations from God, and supernatural manifestations from evil sources.

At some point in time during eternity past, God created a spirit being that was magnificent to behold. He was consecrated and had a covering around the throne of God. He was called by God "the anointed cherub that covereth." He was perfect in all of his ways *until* iniquity was found in him. His name *was* Lucifer, son of the morning.[6] He *is now* called Satan. Through *deception and lies* he persuaded approximately one third of the angels of God to join with him in rebellion *against* God. He and his army of angels lost the battle and were cast from Heaven down to the Earth. Therefore, Satan is also called, "The god of this world."[7]

After Jesus was baptized with the Holy Spirit, He confronted Satan in the desert. Satan brought to the attention of Jesus that all of the kingdoms of this world were given to him. Jesus never refuted that fact.[8] The evil spirits on Earth today are under Satan's control. They work under Satan's control to influence people, to oppress people, and to possess *some* people. They can also influence a variety of social, economic, political, religious, and military institutions here on the Earth. Now, you're probably thinking, "so what does this all have to do with the Gifts, miracles, and workings of the Holy Spirit?" Let's connect the dots by following the scriptures to see.

In his confrontation with God in Heaven, Satan had the audacity to tell God, "I will *be like* the Most High.[9]" That's his objective: *Be like!* From *that* moment until *now*, and even *into the future*, everything Satan does is to "be like" God by *imitating and counterfeiting* the Kingdom and activities of God. Satan imitates the acts of God *through deception.* This includes deceptive supernatural manifestations *that mimic* the Gifts of the Spirit.[10]

In his efforts to "be like" the Most High God, Satan can cause supernatural manifestations to occur through satanic spirits and his human operatives. These manifestations are called "lying signs and wonders." Statues that cry, statues that bleed, people that show nail scars in their hands that ooze blood or oil, dead relatives that appear and vanish, psychic spiritual "operations" on the human body, and operatives with familiar spirits *that mimic the Word of Knowledge* by telling you what has gone on in your life, represent a mere fraction of *supernatural* lying signs and wonders that deceive people *into believing* that these manifestations are of God.[11] They are not! They are works of satanic, deceiving, evil powers. Avoid them!

Jesus Himself warns us through scripture that "false Christs and false Prophets" will arise. Scripture tells us that the *spirit* of anti-Christ *is already* in the world. This spirit is one of deception and it is a prominent characteristic of the last days.[12] Just as there is the Holy Trinity which is composed of God Almighty, the Lord Jesus Christ, and the Holy Spirit, in the future Satan will mimic this by bringing forth an *unholy* trinity. *It* will be composed of Satan himself, who will imitate God, the anti-Christ, who will imitate Jesus Christ, and the False Prophet, who will imitate the Holy Spirit. Their purpose is *total deception* of all people to draw them away from God, and into the kingdom of darkness which results in eternal damnation. All three will receive God's most horrendous and ultimate punishment.[13] And by what method will they have deceived people? *They will deceive people with spectacular lying signs and wonders.*

The spirit of the anti-Christ and the workings of the False Prophet, which scripture tells us is already in the world, are active now. Scripture clearly warns us that *evil* men and seducers shall increase worse and worse, *deceiving*, and being deceived.[14] This is why it is so important that we be able to distinguish between people used by the Holy Spirit to manifest true signs, wonders, and miracles of God, contrasted to people operating under the influence of evil spirits who manifest *lying and false* signs, wonders and miracles. Let's look at a passage of scripture which shows us the differences.

Deceptive Supernatural Activities of Satan Displayed

From scripture we find that an evangelist in the Early Church named Philip went down to a place called Samaria to preach about Jesus Christ, and the Kingdom of God. Before Philip arrived, there was a man in that city named Simon who for a long time used sorcery, and bewitched the city's people to the extent that the people thought that he was "the great power of God." See, *people can be utterly deceived!* He was well experienced in his activity, he had been doing it for a long time, he operated in great power, and he was able to astound people from the least to the greatest. He must have been pretty impressive. So we need to know what he did, and what kind of power enabled him to do it.[15] Let's see the answer.

He *bewitched*, astounded, dazzled, and impressed the people with *sorcery*. Sorcery is an evil practice that has been used throughout history and is still *widely used today*. It is *extremely* subtle. In fact, "soft core" sorcery is currently glamorized in *many* popular children's books, movies, television programs, and games that are presented as harmless fiction and fun. Children are especially targeted because they are very impressionable and their parents are usually clueless that sorcery provides entry level satanic indoctrination. Notice the scriptural terms *bewitched* and *sorcery*. These terms are related to the practice of magic and witchcraft; *the highest levels of satanic activity that can be conducted by humans*.

Sorcery is a method by which sorcerers, witches, and *other operatives* of Satan *delude*, and in fascinating, captivating, and subtle ways *lure* unsuspecting people to unknowingly participate in occult and demonic activities and practices. As an experienced sorcerer, Simon would have had super human power over people and even objects. By using spells, potions, and evil procedures, he could control the free will of people and obtain whatever results he desired while demonstrating *lying* signs and wonders *by the power of evil spirits*. This is how Satan *mimics and counterfeits* the supernatural Gifts of the Holy Spirit, and how he deceives *and control* people. Satan is the originator of lies and he is the master deceiver. Simon also glorified himself by claiming that he was an extraordinary person. Now let's contrast the behavior, activity, and results of Philip's ministry, as compared to the works of Simon.

True Supernatural Activities of God Displayed

In the same city where Satan had a stronghold through Simon, Philip preached about Jesus Christ and things pertaining to the Kingdom of God. The Holy Spirit manifested the Gifts of the Spirit to confirm the words Philip spoke with magnificent supernatural signs, wonders, and miracles.

As a result of Philip's preaching, demon possessed people under the *control* of evil spirits *were set free*. Supernatural healings occurred. Philip didn't glorify himself; he enabled the Holy Spirit to glorify Jesus. Men and women believed on Jesus and were baptized into the Body of Christ. Great joy was brought to the city by Philip. And here's the most interesting accomplishment of all: Simon, a man experienced and knowledgeable in operating in the power of Satan for a long time, realized that the Power of God manifested by the Holy Spirit was real, and far superior to *any* power of Satan. Then, Simon too believed on Jesus.

However, reverting to his old ways, Simon was naïve enough to think that he could *buy* the Power of the Holy Spirit with money so that he could do miracles to benefit himself. He was rebuked and learned otherwise from an apostle called Peter.[16] Never, never, *never*, desire the Gifts of the Holy Spirit to promote a *personal* interest; be it fame, money, power, or anything else!

How *We* can Recognize Supernatural Deception

The presentation of Philip the evangelist compared to the presentation of Simon the sorcerer, when their activities in this city are compared one to another, gives us natural insight from God's Word and several ways in which we can recognize supernatural deception that uses lying signs and wonders performed by people operating under the control of evil spirits. When compared to true supernatural signs and wonders manifested by the Gifts of the Holy Spirit through people like Philip, under the control of the Holy Spirit, the contrast and differences are obvious and profound. Here's what we see, and here's what we should watch for to confirm that the manifestations we see *are* of the Holy Spirit.

The supernatural spiritual Gifts of the Holy Spirit will always glorify Jesus, never man. The Holy Spirit will draw people to Jesus, never to man. The Holy Spirit will set people free from demonic control and influence, not keep them in bondage. Ministers and people through whom the Gifts of the Spirit manifest should always deify and point the way to Jesus Christ, not to themselves or anyone *other* than Jesus. The Gifts of the Spirit will always be a blessing to people, and their community. The Gifts of the Spirit will always be consistent with the Word of God, confirm the Word of God, and glorify the Lord Jesus Christ and God *only*.[17] **Any supernatural manifestation coming through people *devoid* of these qualities should be suspected of *being deceptive, false, or trickery,* coming from a *source other* than the Holy Spirit of God!**

Other Forms of Spiritual Deception

An insidious and dangerous type of *supernatural deception,* totally despised by God and frequently encountered today, is perversion of the Divine Vocal Communication Gifts. Satan has been active in this area throughout history but is intensifying his activities in these areas during these particular times. The Gift *most often perverted* in this group *is personal prophecy.* God abhors those who tell someone something about *their* past, present, or future, using *His Name* when what *they* said *didn't come from Him!* The best insight we can receive regarding this problem is found in scripture.[18] God knows that the perversion of *one* Gift, can damage the credibility of *other* Gifts of the Spirit.

Satanic supernatural practices have not changed. They've just become slicker and more deceptive to match the times in which we are living. Be aware of the deceptive *methods* that are used. Never forget that it is the Holy Spirit and the Word of God who reveals to us *the nature and operations of God,* and the supreme power we have through Christ. Likewise, the Word of God and the Holy Spirit also reveal to us *the nature and operations of Satan and his* methods of spiritual deception. Scripture calls satanic methods of deception "the wiles of the devil" and tells us that they *can* be stood against![19]

Spiritual deception in the form of religion is a *vicious* but subtle satanic stronghold. We must beware of religious institutions, cults, and people that masquerade with the Name of Jesus, but whose gospel and doctrines are not of Christ. They may look good, sound good, and have huge followings. Many honor the Lord Jesus Christ with their lips, but *their hearts are far* from Him. Given the times in which we live and the times *that shall come*, we must know the

Word of God and ask the Holy Spirit to expose those whose teachings distort and corrupt the Word of God, or who use deceptive supernatural manifestations from sources that are evil. [20]

Just because an organization calls itself a "church" does not make it a true church of God. Also, Jesus Himself clearly states that there *are people* in some "churches of God" that worship with satanic practices.[21] Some satanic practices are so subtle, and appear to be so harmless, that even Believers can be deceived unless they really know the Word of God, and depend upon the Holy Spirit to expose satanic deception to them. In addition, there are numerous "churches" on Earth today that are actually called churches of Satan and operate accordingly. They have their own "ministers," bibles, and they worship Satan. This comes as no surprise to *those who are knowledgeable* because scripture from the Word of God tells us that Satan, a spirit being, is transformed into an angel of light, and that it is no great thing that he transforms *his ministers* to *be as* ministers of righteousness.[22] This is the highest form and level of spiritual deception.

The Essential Combination

All modes and manners of *spiritual deception*, whether supernatural or not, are tools of Satan designed to separate and keep people from God. Satan knows that by accepting the blood bought sacrifice of God's Son, the resurrected Lord Jesus Christ, mankind can accomplish eternal salvation and union with God.

Remember, the Word of God is Truth, and the Holy Spirit is the Spirit of Truth. It is the Holy Spirit who guides us into all truth and therefore enables us to

clearly perceive spiritual deception because spiritual deception is contrary to God's Word. So, by knowing the Word of God and having the Holy Spirit, *you too are knowledgeable* and well equipped to identify *any type of spiritual deception.* Knowing the Word of God and having the Holy Spirit *is the essential combination we must have for us to not be deceived!* The supporting scriptures below related to these matters are important to know.[23] Please read them!

Supporting Scriptures:
How to Identify Supernatural Deception
Please read the scriptures

---

1 Ex 7:10-12
2 Deut 18:9-12, 2 Chr 33:6, Lev 20:27, Dan 2:2, Mal 3:5
3 2 Cor 11:13-15, 2 Pet 2:1, 1 Ti 4:1, 2 Ti 4:2,3, Jn17:17, Jn 16:13, Rev 18:23
4 Jn 8:44
5 2 Ki 6:8-12
6 Eze 28:12-19, Is 14:12-15
7 2 Cor 4:3, 4, Mt 4:8,9
8 Lk 10:18, 2 Cor 4:4, Mk 1:11-13, Mt 4:8
9 Is 14:14
10 Mt 7:15, Mt 24:11
11 2 Th 2:7-11
12 Mt 24:24, 1 Jn 4:1-3, 1 Jn 2:18
13 Rev 20:10
14 2 Ti 3:13
15 Acts 8:5-13
16 Acts 8:18-24
17 Acts 8:12, 8:8, Mk 16:20, Jn16:13,14
18 Jer 14:14,15, 29:9, Eze 13:2-8,
19 Eph 6:11
20 2 Cor 2:17, Isa 29:13, Mt 15:8, Rom 3:13, Eze 33:31
21 Rev 2:9, 13, 14, 20.

[22] 2 Cor 11:13-15

[23] Mk 13:21,22, 2 Cor11:3, 4, Is 30:8-11, Gal 1:6-9, 2 Jn 1:7, 2 Ti 4:2-4, Jn 3:16, Acts 4:10-12, Heb 5:13,14, Jn 17:17, Jn 14:16,17

CHAPTER FIFTEEN

THE POWER OF THE HOLY SPIRIT

This book is about the Holy Spirit, His Gifts, and His Power; *all* of which are available *for you* through the Lord Jesus Christ. Except for love, there is *nothing* comparable to the Power of the Holy Spirit. We have given considerable attention to the *Holy Spirit* and *His Gifts*. Now let's give attention to *His Power*. In doing so, we shall discover that His Power is fully integrated and associated with the Holy Spirit Himself, the Gifts of the Spirit, the Lord Jesus Christ, God the Father, the Word of God, and Spirit-filled Believers. Then we shall see *how* His Power is released and what the results are. *This Power cannot be delegated for use except by the authority of the Lord Jesus Christ.*[1]

There are many kinds of power that we are familiar with. There's political power, mechanical power, human physical power, solar power, military power, and numerous other types of power of which we are aware. We are aware of these types of power because it is power that is confined to, and operates within our understanding of time, space, and matter in this realm. It is power that can be understood by our human senses. Such power has *no effect* in any invisible or unseen spiritual realm. There *are* unseen spiritual realms that *are not* limited to time, space, or matter as we know it, and there are different types of power in those realms. But, there is mighty Supreme power that can affect *those* realms, and *this* realm in which we live. This Supreme power is above all types of power in *this or any other* realm. It is the greatest of all power that ever has been, that is, or that shall ever be. It existed before the beginning of time, and it is eternal. This power is the Power of the Holy Spirit of God. We're now going to learn some things about this Supreme Power.

God anointed Jesus with the Holy Spirit *and* with power.[2] The Holy Spirit and power are two separate entities which describe *how* God enabled Jesus to become Christ, meaning the Anointed One. The Holy Spirit is a Divine Person. The word power in this context means ability, might, and strength *associated with wonderful work*. The word anointed refers to a special endowment, provision, or furnishing that is given or bestowed. So Almighty God bestowed upon, gave to, and furnished Jesus with a special provision. That provision was the Divine Person of the Holy Spirit and *the Spirit's* ability, might, and power to do wonderful works. Wow! Read this again because it applies to us too. Let's examine several examples showing how the Holy Spirit manifests His power.

Power for Life and Godliness

If you were to do a comprehensive study on the power of the Holy Spirit, you would discover that His Power is the power of the Gospel of Jesus Christ, the power by which we are saved. It is the power that was involved at the conception of the Lord Jesus Christ, in the Virgin Mary, by the Holy Spirit. It is the power Jesus gave to His disciples over *all* devils, to cure diseases, to preach the Kingdom of God, and to heal the sick. It is the power that operates with the Gifts of the Spirit.

This is the same power that resurrected Jesus from the dead, and that will raise His Believers from the dead. It is the power of the Kingdom of God. It is the power that enabled the apostles to speak the Word of God boldly and give witness of the resurrection of Jesus Christ. It is the power by which Jesus upholds *all things* by His Word. It is the power that can deliver *anyone* from *any type* of bondage, addiction, or destructive condition. It is the power He commands us to receive and it is the power through which we are kept. We can see that this mighty power of God, executed by the Holy Spirit, is fully integrated into all things. Gloriously, it is *according* to *this* divine power that *we have* all things that pertain to life and godliness.[3]

This Power is Within Us

Before seeing how the power of God can be released *by us*, it is important to understand that if we belong to Jesus Christ, and we are baptized with the Holy Spirit, all of the power and attributes of God are within us. Let's prove this by scripture.

Christ in us is the hope of glory. He dwells in us through the Holy Spirit *as* the Spirit of Christ. Before going to the cross Jesus prayed to the Father that we may all be one. He prayed that as He was one in the Father, and the Father was one in Him, that we may be one in Them: He in us and God in Him, that we may be made perfect in one.[4] Now, here's what's important for us to understand.

After His completed work of the cross and ascension into Heaven, God made Jesus both Lord and Christ. Therefore He is the Savior with all authority and power. But here is the main thing. God placed into Jesus Christ bodily, *all* of the fullness of the Godhead. In other words, everything that God is and has is now also in Jesus Christ. Likewise, everything the Holy Spirit is and has is also now in Jesus Christ. And Jesus Christ now is and has everything He ever had or will have, and He now is everything that He ever was, or will ever be. He is the same yesterday, today, and forever.[5]

Now here's how we *know* that all of the power and attributes of God are in us. In Christ Jesus dwells all of the fullness of the Godhead bodily. *And we are complete in Him!* Therefore, as He is so are we in this world. How is Jesus Christ in us? He is in us as the Spirit of Christ by the Holy Spirit! Furthermore, a king resides wherever his kingdom is. The Kingdom of God is within us. Therefore, Jesus with all of His power and ability resides over His Kingdom that is within us. Hence, we have all of the nature and power of God, which is resident in the Kingdom of God, available to us and to be used through us, because it is in us. We are limited *only by our own ability* to tap into this power. The more we allow the Holy Spirit to reveal to us the totality of Jesus Christ and who we are *in Him*, the more we *meditate* on the Word of God day and night, the more we understand *our covenant* with God through Jesus Christ, *and the more we worship and fellowship with Him,* the more *ability* we have to tap into this reservoir of power that is within us.[6] This is important to know, and wonderful to understand.

How We Release the Power

We release the power of God the same way *He* does: through words. *The power is released when we* ***speak words*** *in faith,* especially God's Word. His Word is *powerful*. His

Word is spirit. His Word is alive. His Word is life. His Word is health. His Word is true. His Word is so important that He magnifies it above *all* His Name, and His Word is forever settled in Heaven.[7] Releasing God's power by *speaking* His Word is what I call power through *active faith*. We can also release His power through absolute and total faith and trust in God *alone*. This I call releasing God's power through *passive faith*.

Power through Active Faith

We see that in the beginning when God created the heavens and the Earth, that the Earth was enveloped in darkness. God *spoke* the word for light to be, and by *the power* of the Holy Spirit light was brought forth. Nine times God *said* what He wanted to occur, and nine times *the power* of the Holy Spirit brought into being the words God *spoke*.[8] This is the release of God's power through *active faith*. Let's examine several other examples where the Holy Spirit performed words that were spoken. Jesus is our best example.

Jesus *Demonstrates* Releasing the Power

On a certain occasion Jesus, who of course was fully anointed with the Holy Spirit and power, and His disciples were in a ship going across a lake. The scripture informs us that suddenly there arose a *great* storm of wind. The wind was so powerful that it stirred up the waves and caused water to fill the ship carrying them. During all of this, Jesus was asleep in the back of the ship and had to be awakened by His disciples who were afraid that they were all going to perish. Now let's watch what Jesus did.[9]

He *rebuked* the wind *and said* to the sea, "Peace, be

still." In essence, He said to the elements that could have destroyed them, *"Stop it!"* Scripture says the wind ceased and there was a great calm. The disciples were in awe and feared exceedingly after seeing this, and in essence said to each other, "What kind of man *is this?* Even the wind and the sea obey Him!" The answer to their question is this: Jesus was a man filled with the Holy Spirit. During that time of danger He spoke words and told the elements *to be still.* He *believed* the words He spoke would come to pass. What He spoke came to pass because the words He spoke in faith released the necessary power of the Holy Spirit to make the wind and sea be calm. *The Holy Spirit releases power to perform words spoken in faith.*

Here's what's very interesting to notice. Jesus asked His disciples, "Where is *your* faith?" Now, after such a dangerous episode and experience, which they had encountered, why would Jesus ask them *a question like that?* As we discover from scripture *what Jesus did and taught* in the passage coming up, we get a clue.

It appears to me that Jesus not only asked a question, but in that question He also implied a statement. The implied statement seems to have been: why didn't *you speak to the problem*, like I did, and *stop it yourself!* So, let's get some insight from the scriptures and examples that Jesus gave in these passages.

These passages are essential for us to examine because in them, Jesus gives *a demonstration* and *follow-up explanations* to explain faith. We know this teaching is also for us because Jesus made it clear that it even applies to "whosoever."

It appears that Jesus wanted us to understand that what He did, the disciples could do, and with our spiritual faith we could and should do the same thing and achieve astounding results.

One evening Jesus and twelve of His disciples left a Temple in Jerusalem and headed for a city called Bethany. The next day when they were leaving Bethany, Jesus was hungry. At a good distance away He saw a fig tree with leaves. He went over to the tree to see if it had figs on it. There were none. Yet, there were leaves on the tree! In the Mid East, when a fig tree has leaves, the fig tree is supposed to have figs. Jesus knew this. He also knew that something was wrong with *that* tree. It was deceiving those who needed its fruit, and it was perverting the natural laws of nature that God established. So Jesus decided to destroy it. Let's see *how* Jesus destroyed it.[10]

Jesus didn't tell His disciples, "Boys, go get me an axe so I can chop this tree down." He didn't set the tree on fire and burn it up. Jesus destroyed the fig tree by speaking in faith what He believed would come to pass. He spoke words through His mouth that were the same as cursing the tree to death. What He desired happened, because the next day the tree was seen dried up from the roots and withered away. According to Jesus, we have the same ability to release the same power of God that He did. *He tells us* ***we can*** *do it,* then *He tells us* ***how to do it***.

Jesus Tells Us *How* to Release the Power of God

First of all Jesus says, "Have faith in God." Here, He's not only talking about believing and trusting in God, but also to use our faith like God uses His. This kind of faith, as we have seen, is faith that releases the power of the

Holy Spirit. I call this *active faith.*[A] It involves speaking words and expecting the words spoken to come to pass. Remember now, Jesus is explaining this process right after He had just *demonstrated it* by cursing the fig tree. Here's what's astounding and great to know! In His teaching, Jesus tells us that this ability belongs *to whosoever, for whatsoever! Whosoever* applied to His disciples, applies to us, and applies to *anyone. Whatsoever* applies to *anything*, as long as it doesn't violate the Word of God. Read the supporting scriptures of these passages for yourself.[11] Right now I'm going to break the scriptural passage down so what Jesus said can be easily understood.

In essence, this is what Jesus Himself tells us. Whosoever shall say; that means to use your tongue and speak out of your mouth.[B] To this mountain; that means to the obstacle or problem confronting you. Be removed and be cast into the sea; that means go, vanish, and disappear to a far away deep place. And shall not doubt in his heart; that means don't be uncertain, don't waver. But believe those things he says shall come to pass; that means be absolutely convinced that what you said, and continue to say, *will* occur. He shall *have whatsoever* he *says*; in other words, *what he continually demands to occur!* In more times than I can remember I have made demands in the Name of Jesus Christ and seen fabulous results. Let me share several instances with you.

[A] **There is another level of faith that is equally as profound. I call it *passive faith.***

[B] **This demonstrates the power of words spoken by the tongue. See: Prov 18:21, Prov 12:18, Jas 3:3-10. Rev 1:16, Rev 2:16, Rev 19:15**

Power Released in the Life and Ministry of the Author

While ministering in a university church facility leased for our services, the Holy Spirit gave me a Word of Knowledge that a woman in attendance had a lump in her breast. I believe she was scheduled for surgery, but don't recall for sure. The Holy Spirit did not reveal to me the type of mass it was; it could have been a tumor or it could have been a cyst. When I revealed this information to the people, a lady in the back of the auditorium stood to her feet. Despite the distance, I pointed my finger at the lump *and spoke to it.* I cursed it in the Name of Jesus Christ by telling it to dry up and die. I then commanded it to be uprooted and go from her body.

Then I inquired if there was a nurse in attendance. There was. I requested the nurse and the lady ministered to, to go to "the ladies room" and get the results. Several minutes later both women ran back into the auditorium full of joy and praises to God. The lump had completely and totally disappeared! In this situation however, I had an advantage. I *knew* the power of the Holy Spirit was going to be released. I was sure of the results the moment I spoke commands to the mass. Why? Because *this* problem was revealed to me by the Holy Spirit who, when I minister, *always* heals *what He reveals to me*. I have *never* seen Him fail to heal what *He* reveals when the person *wants* to be healed. But what about situations where my own *personal faith* is necessary?

One afternoon our daughter was suffering from a severe migraine headache that *would not* respond to *any* medication she was taking. I went to her home, put my left hand on her head, *spoke to the pain in the Name of Jesus Christ*, and commanded the pain *to go. It did!* However it did resist twice before *completely* leaving. *My faith* was solid because I was doing what Jesus *said to do*. The words spoken *to the headache*, in the Name of Jesus Christ, released the power of the Holy Spirit who then performed the words that were spoken. I have discovered that sometimes however, it's a little more difficult to get the desired results you want when *your own* personal faith is required. This is especially true if the person you are trying to help is full of doubt and unbelief but *pretends* to be otherwise.

So, when we *speak* words according to the scripturally sound principles that Jesus taught, we can release the *power* of God to bring forth any blessing or overcome any obstacle *we* are addressing! We have this power available. Now we know how to use it. Use it yourself, because Jesus said it can be used by *whosoever*.

Don't Be Confused

A lot of people become confused by thinking that Bible verse twenty-two of Mark chapter eleven relates only to verses twenty-four, twenty-five, and twenty-six because of the word "therefore." In this entire passage of scripture, from Mark 11:22 to Mark 11:26, Jesus is speaking about two *different types* of prayer, but using principles that are *similar* to both types. In verse twenty-three Jesus is talking about executing faith like God does: make a demand by speaking words. Therefore Jesus is saying, by speaking words *make a demand* in *His* Name, The Name of Jesus, *and He, Jesus*, would do it.[12] In verses twenty-four and five, Jesus is talking about trusting and *asking the Father* to do something in *His Name*, meaning the Name of Jesus, *and the Father* would do it![13]

These are two different types of prayer: One type makes a demand while the other type makes a request. Both types depend upon similar principles: believe those things *you are saying* shall come to pass when you *make a demand* in the Name of Jesus, *and*, believe *you receive* what you desire *when you pray* as you make a *request* from the Father in the Name of Jesus. In *both* cases it is the Holy Spirit, by His power, who brings forth the results.

Power through Passive Faith

The other type of faith that is extremely powerful when it is released is what I call *passive faith.* This kind of faith occurs when you put *absolute and total trust* in God to give you the victory over whatever condition, situation, or circumstance that may be confronting you. This is another aspect of what Jesus meant when He said, "Have faith in God."

How to Release the Power of Passive Faith

When you realize that there is absolutely nothing *you* can do to change your situation, and you intentionally cast the whole of your cares upon God and trust Him to act on your behalf to deliver you from the situation, whatever it may be, *passive faith begins.*[14] This is simple child-like belief, trust in, depending upon and relying upon God *alone.*[C] Here is *how* we release the power of passive faith: cast all of the care, worry, and anxieties of the problem, the problem itself and things associated with the problem, onto Jesus Christ.

[C] **Read the New Jersey Special Assignment**

After casting our cares on Him, God then takes up our battle and wins the victory for us. The Holy Spirit, by His power, performs the work and brings the results. All we have to do is to continually thank God for the results we desire as though it's done.

The first time I *totally* engaged in this type of faith occurred when we conducted our first public ministry assignment. The onslaughts of satanic hindrances were so numerous and overwhelming at critical times, that I realized there was *nothing* that I could do *except* to cast those burdens onto the Lord. I simply asked Him to take care of them for me, and then without worry, but trust in Him, *I just forgot about them.* As I did this, I discovered that the results were astounding victories. Our sovereign God released His power on my behalf because of my total and complete trust in Him and dependence on Him. This is awesome, but it is the kind of faith many mature Christians *limit* themselves to. This kind of faith should not, however, be substituted for the God kind of faith where words are spoken to obtain the things Jesus has already secured for us on the cross, or the work of faith God wants *us to do* using *our faith* ourselves.[15]

In the final analysis we see that the power of the Holy Spirit is released on our behalf in two distinct ways: *By God Himself* when we totally relinquish our concerns to Him, and totally trust Him to resolve them for us, and *by us* when we speak *to* the problem using words in a manner consistent with the teachings of Jesus.

The Power and the Gifts of the Spirit

The awesome supernatural *power* of the Holy Spirit appears to be automatically released with the manifestations of the Gift of Faith, Gifts of Healings, and the Working of Miracles. The same seems to be true in many instances, *but indirectly*, with the Word of Knowledge, the Word of Wisdom, and the Discerning of spirits; depending upon the purpose and manner in which these Gifts are manifested.

Take healing for instance. With the Gifts of Healings, the release of the power of the Holy Spirit is direct, sovereign, and self evident. On the other hand, should a Word of Knowledge reveal a specific diseased condition, the power of the Holy Spirit *would not* be released to heal that condition until the condition was addressed by the person through whom the power of the Holy Spirit is operating.

It is my desire that this insight regarding the Power of the Holy Spirit will further inspire you to receive the Lord Jesus Christ as your personal Savior and to be baptized with the Holy Spirit if you haven't already done so. Then, *if it is your desire*, pray for the Holy Spirit to use you with His Gifts and Power to reveal the Lord Jesus Christ, glorify the Lord Jesus Christ, demonstrate the Kingdom of God, and be a blessing to others in new ways.

A Time To Refresh Again

Once more, the Holy Spirit has graciously given us considerable insight and information. Some pertained to His marvelous Divine Gifts of Power and Ability, His Gifts of Divine Vocal Communication, and Supernatural Voices that can be heard. We also learned how to identify dangerous Supernatural Deception of evil powers, and saw that the Holy Spirit's own spectacular Divine Power is far greater and superior. What we've covered has been extensive and awe-inspiring. But there are still some fascinating subjects and areas of scriptural and real life experiences to be read. I believe this is a good time to relax again, meditate on what you've read, and review the supporting scriptures. Remember to pray and expect the Holy Spirit to give you further understanding through the supporting scriptures on all that you have read thus far.

When we continue, we will follow several unique Special Assignments given to me where the Holy Spirit and

His Power were greatly needed, and manifested beautifully. Most importantly, we are going to discover the Secret of Worship as it relates to the Gifts of the Spirit. *This is the greatest treasure we will learn.* Then, we will learn some Essential Steps that we can take to put ourselves into a greater position to be used by the Holy Spirit and His Gifts.

From the Concluding Remarks, you will see that you too can be wonderfully used by the Holy Spirit, His Gifts and Power. Finally, be sure to read the Prayer of Blessings that I believe the Holy Spirit gave me to bless you, then read the Special Statement and Special Request on page 250.

Supporting Scriptures:
The Power of the Holy Spirit
Please read the scriptures

---

[1] Mt 28:18,19, Lk 10:19, Jn 16:7, Acts 1:4,5,7, Rom 15:19, 1 Cor 2:4,5

[2] 1 Cor 2 :4, Acts 10:38, Jn 1:32-34, Mt 16:16, 1 Col 1:24, 1 Thess 1:5

[3] Rom 1:16, 1 Cor 1:18, Lk 1:35, 9:1, 10:19, 1 Th 1:5, 1 Cor 6:14, Mk 9:1, Acts 4:31,33, Heb 1:3, Acts1:4-8, 1 Pet 1:5, 2 Pet 1:2

[4] Col 1:27, Rom 8:9, Jn 17:21,23

[5] Acts2:36, Col 2:9, Heb 13:8

[6] Col 2:10, 1 Jn 4:17, Rom 8:9, Lk 17:20,21

[7] Heb 4:12, Jn 6:63, Prov 4:22, Jn 17:17, Ps 138:2, Ps 119:89

[8] Gen 1:1-26

[9] Lk 8:22-25

[10] Mk 11:11-14, 19-21

[11] Mk 11:22,23

[12] Jn 14:13,14

[13] Jn 16:23

[14] Mk 11:22, 1 Pe 5:7

[15] Mt 17:20, 21:21, Lk 8:25

SPECIAL ASSIGNMENTS

Now that you have some fairly good insight about the Holy Spirit, the Inward Witness, the Gifts of the Spirit, and His Power, I will share with you several *special assignments* given to me by the Holy Spirit that glorified the Lord Jesus Christ, demonstrated the Kingdom of God, and proved to be a blessing to others. One assignment is called the New Jersey Assignment, the other, the Florida Assignment.

You will notice how various Gifts and activities of the Holy Spirit performed like a grand symphony culminating with spectacular results. You will notice the interconnection between the Inward Witness, prayer, obedience, faith, and the Gifts of the Holy Spirit. The Gifts of the Spirit sometimes manifested individually, and at other times flowed together in beautiful harmony. You will behold the glory of God on many levels, be more informed, and also be inspired to see how the wonderful Holy Spirit can work through a person.

CHAPTER SIXTEEN

THE NEW JERSEY ASSIGNMENT

At some point in time all of us must take that first step regarding any new endeavor. This is an account of such a step. It is an exposition of the very first *special assignment* given to me by the Holy Spirit. It discloses the enormous challenges that confronted me as a brand new minister of the Gospel and reveals how the Power of God overcame powers of darkness that sought to prevent my very first *public ministry event*. Everything connected with this first mission required my absolute and total dependence upon the Lord. Although the account of this assignment is lengthy, it is very informative and exciting.

Early in the Spring about two years after making a commitment to the Lord to minister the Gospel, the Holy Spirit began to place into my heart a desire to hold three days of public healing services in Newark, New Jersey. That's where I grew up. The more I prayed about the event, the more the Holy Spirit seemed to indicate, "Yes, hold it there in November!" However there was an *overwhelming* problem: I had never done anything like this before.

I didn't have any procedural knowledge, staff, or personnel to help. I had no contacts, equipment, supplies, prayer warriors, music minister, or money. Nothing! I recall explaining the situation to the Lord and saying, "Lord, I'm supposed to be holding a big time meeting in a situation like this? You 'gotta' be kidding me!" He wasn't. So I did the only thing I knew *to do*: pray! I really wanted some strong confirmation about all of this.

Shortly afterwards, my wife and I met and became friendly with a couple who had recently graduated from a local Bible school. We informed them about what I perceived the Lord wanted us to do in New Jersey. They became excited and asked to join with us. My immediate answer was, "Yes, join us!" They were from New Jersey! They then told *one* of their friends who was a prayer warrior about this assignment. She was *excited about the mission*, wanted to join us, *and* wanted to organize a group of Believers to pray for us. She too, was from New Jersey! They all proved to be great friends full of faith, prayer, support, and encouragement. Things were beginning to come together and it seemed as though the Lord was *confirming* what the Holy Spirit was leading me to do. But in all honesty, at *that* time I still wasn't full of rock solid faith about the whole thing. However my conduct displayed a classic example of being led by the Inward Witness through the Holy Spirit. I was trusting in the Lord with all of my heart, not leaning upon *my* understanding, but acknowledging *Him* in all of my ways and I watched Him actually bring things to pass.

As time passed, small amounts of proceeds for the mission began trickling in from unexpected sources. About four to six weeks prior to our departure I noticed more intense fervor in my prayers. Suddenly, the Gifts of the Holy Spirit began to manifest when I prayed! During one prayer session the Holy Spirit showed me the beautiful inside of a Jewish Temple with round walls, its dome-shaped ceiling with a gorgeous Star of David, striking pews and carpet. During another prayer session, The Holy Spirit gave me a vision of the name of a man written in cursive. Both revelations were Words of Knowledge. The Holy Spirit also gave me a highly *symbolic* vision through the Word of Wisdom. In this vision, I saw myself in water surrounded by large numbers of big snakes. Then I saw myself walking up out of the water onto dry land with my feet *in boots* up to my knees. It wasn't until the trip was over that the Holy Spirit gave me the meaning of this vision. All of the Gifts of the Spirit which manifested through me during this period of time occurred during different sessions *while I was praying*. It was evident that the Lord was elevating me to a higher spiritual level.

Then, a week or so before our departure to New Jersey two significant events occurred. One event gave me *total confirmation* that God had *prearranged* this assignment. The other demonstrated how *God provided* contacts and greatly needed resources at a critical time. We shall see the awesome Power of God battle and overcome the forces and influence of evil that tried to *stop* His plans and purpose for this ministry. I think you'll find all of these events quite insightful.

The Confirmation

One evening our prayer leader took my wife and me to visit a pastor whom she knew well, but whom we had never seen or met. He was knowledgeable about the civil and legal factors that must be complied with in order to conduct the kind of public meetings we were to have. This pastor then disclosed to us what we felt was the most stunning part of our visit with him.

He revealed that he saw me walking down an aisle at a prayer seminar eight months earlier and that the Spirit of God said to him, "See that man? I'm going to send him to you, and when I do, I want you to help him." Then, the pastor said that the moment he opened the door and saw me, the Spirit of God said to him, "Here he is." He had expected to see me, but he just didn't know when.

This is a superb example of the Word of Wisdom that operated *through that pastor*. The pastor didn't know me or know my name. Now, after being introduced and brought up to speed regarding our concerns, he was extremely helpful. The words he spoke regarding what the Spirit of God had said to him long before the Holy Spirit *had put this assignment into my heart* caused me *to know* without a doubt that God had set this assignment up and that we were doing God's perfect Will. This was comforting confirmation to me, and my faith was *hardened like steel*.

The First Provision

Shortly afterwards, a remarkable event occurred. A minister I had met several years earlier was driving from North Carolina on his way north and dropped by to visit with us unannounced. I thought his visit was unusual since we had not communicated with each other for more than a year. After acquainting ourselves with each other again, he asked me what the Lord was having me to do. I told him about the assignment. He asked when I was leaving. I said, "Friday!" He said, "No wonder the Lord told me to hurry up and get here." He then reached to the inside of his coat pocket and gave me an envelope containing cash. We prayed over it, thanked God, and he left.

We had previously *reserved* one way tickets to get three of us to New Jersey but didn't have the money to buy them. After the minister left, we opened the envelope, counted the money, and discovered that to the penny, the cash was *exactly* the amount we needed to buy the tickets!

This minister was sensitive to the Holy Spirit who *must* have told him to get a certain amount of money to us quickly. I had heard of God providing *for others* like this, but this time He was providing *for me!*

First Essential Contact

Later during the week, following a time of late night prayer, the Holy Spirit instructed me to call a former college classmate *right away*. I had not communicated with him in years and I was shocked to be told to call him because the hour was so late. So I said to the Lord, "Lord, it's almost one o'clock in the morning this guy's time. He'll think I'm nuts calling him this late at night. And besides, I haven't spoken to the man in over twenty years! I don't even know where he lives any more, and I certainly don't have his phone number. Nonetheless, if You say do it, I'll do it."

After calling telephone information to get his number, I called him. To my surprise he was still up. Instead of being peeved for getting such a late call, he was delighted to hear from me and wanted to know where I was and what I was doing. I quickly cut to the chase and told him what I was now doing *as a minister* and that I perceived the Lord was sending me to New Jersey to minister. I also told him that *it was the Lord* who instructed me to contact him even though it was so late. He said, "Wow, this sounds like the kind of stuff my wife's into.[A] Let me have you talk to her!" Within seconds his wife was on the phone and I was

---

[A] **I utterly detest *any* activity or work for God being referred to as *"stuff."* Such comments are grossly irreverent and disrespectful, even when used in ignorance and thoughtlessness. However, this man was a "babe in Christ" at that particular time, who later became a tremendous Believer.**

explaining why the Lord was sending us there. Her response was, "I'd like to be involved! I'd love for you to speak with my pastor. Would it be okay if I set it up so you could meet him when you get here?" Obviously I agreed. When the call was over, I shook my head in amazement. God knew exactly what He was doing. All I needed to do was shut up and do what He told me to do by the Spirit. This was another confirmation that we were in God's perfect will and my faith was strengthened even more!

First Satanic Hindrance Second Essential Contact

It was at this point that the powers of darkness began their manifestation to interrupt the plans and purposes of God for the ministry. Here's what happened: our early morning flight from Oklahoma to New Jersey had long delays and we didn't arrive until after 12:30 P.M. We were scheduled to meet her pastor at 11:00 A.M! However, our meeting with him was rescheduled and we were hurriedly taken directly to his home after arriving at the airport. This is when we learned that the pastor was also an apostle. As you will see later *this was very significant*.

The Apostle's home was in the aristocratic area of West Orange; secluded, spacious lawn, beautiful trees, it was *very* nice. After entering, we were escorted to a large reception area for guests. The Apostle came in, we were introduced to him, and then we all sat down and engaged in conversation. After about fifteen minutes he arose, thanked me for coming and expressed his best wishes for our success. I thought to myself, "It's not going to end like this. Not without prayer!" So I asked his permission for me to pray. Permission was granted. After prayer his comment went from, "Best wishes for your success," to "If I can do anything to help you, let me know." That was an enormous change in attitude that I really appreciated. I thanked him and then we drove to my mother's home where we had food, shelter, a place to stay, and a place where our team could hold meetings.

Our first staff meeting occurred at 7:30 P.M. later that evening. A Word of Knowledge manifested *at the beginning of the meeting* and a new team member was set totally free of pain that had attacked her body. Because this occurred so early before the services even began, the Holy Spirit seemed to indicate that He was going to move and operate through us in a tremendous way. We were all excited and our faith was at a very high level.

The people at the meeting were my first cousin, her co-worker, whose name it was that I had seen written in the Spirit and the one God provided to conduct the services, his wife, our advance preparation couple, our prayer leader, my mother, my wife and I. Everybody was informed as to what had been accomplished and all of the logistical needs that still needed to be met. Our advance preparation couple had worked hard to secure a facility, arrange public advertising, and recruit a music minister who happened to graduate from the famous Julliard School of Music in New York. She too was a former Newark resident. However, she needed a piano.

Major Needs Provided

The next day, Saturday, the majority of my activity involved hours of effort to find a place that would rent us a piano for the services. My efforts were all in vain. Then the Holy Spirit, through the Inward Witness, *led me* to call the

Apostle to see *if he knew where* we could rent a piano. I was glad that I was sitting down when he responded. He said, "No, I don't know where you can get a piano, but would an organ be okay? I've got an organ you can use!" Then he continued, "What *else* do you need?" My answer was, "Yes, the organ is great. We also need microphones, chairs, a podium…" He interrupted, "I have all of that. Tell you what, I'll just send one of my crews over there to set you up with every thing."

It turned out that in fulfilling his calling and ministry as an apostle, he traveled all over the country preaching the Gospel in tents to establish churches. He had several crews and a two ton truck that carried everything he needed to conduct meetings anywhere in the nation. *Now* it appeared to us that everything was in order and ready to go. The God who supplies all of our needs according to His riches in glory by Christ Jesus was aware of our needs and supplied them *all*. This was another confirmation to us that we were in God's perfect will and everybody's faith was strengthened even more! But unknown to us, Satan had a devastating ace up his sleeve intending to *stop* us. He thought he was going to perform his act on the upcoming Monday.

First Satanic Attack
God's Victory

Early Monday morning, my wife and I and our advance couple who had retained the facility, went to the YMCA to inspect the area that they had reserved for the meetings. They obtained a large room but it had one problem: it *leaked very badly* when it rained because of a large hole in the roof. We went to the Office of the Administrator in order to "tie up loose ends." It was at this point that Satan let his arrows go to try to *stop* the ministry. Here's what happened.

After greeting and shaking my hand, the Administrator with cold candor, informed me that we could not hold our meetings there. She felt that the "Y" was not "the proper place" to hold "religious" meetings, and she indicated that her decision could not be changed! Let's get this straight. This *woman*, felt it was improper, to hold *Christian* religious *services*, at the Young *Men's Christian* Association facility. To me, *that* took gall! The rest of the team was devastated.

I asked her if she realized that months of preparation, expense, advertising, and expectation of the people in the community was involved. I asked if this kind of disruption, just three days before the events were to start, was the right thing to do. I asked if she understood the impact of such a decision, at this late stage, on the efforts that had been made. She said she was sorry. I was not furious at the lady, *but I was at Satan. She* seemed like a real nice lady. Through the Discerning of spirits, by the Holy Spirit working through me, I *knew* there was satanic influence behind her sudden actions. With faith that came from somewhere within me that I didn't know existed, I looked this lady straight in the eyes and *boldly* told her without batting an eye, "This *will not* stand. We *will* hold our meetings here." We left and I instructed the whole team to just pray while I too would go before the Lord in prayer.

Later that afternoon, my mother came to me with a recommendation. She, herself, wanted to contact a long time family friend who at *that* time was a popular state senator, and explain the situation to him. He and I used to play together as kids. I approved. She called, and within an hour, the problem was solved! We *would* have the Lord's meetings there at that "Y" after all. By the way, I had the privilege of praying for that state senator when he ran for Congress. He is now one of the finest and God-fearing Congressmen in the United States Congress.

Last Satanic Attack God's Victory

Though Satan thus far had failed with his every effort, he *desperately* wanted *to stop* these meetings from occurring. So he prepared *one more* arrow to shoot, this time at me *personally*. He started his attack late on Tuesday evening. By Wednesday, the day before the first service, my voice was *nearly* gone. By Thursday, *the day of* the first service, my voice was *completely* gone. Eating throat lozenges and beaten egg whites combined did no good. Once again, I totally depended upon the Lord and did what I only *could* do: pray *in whispers*. I couldn't imagine God bringing us this far, shattering every obstacle, and then have me get up in front of the people *at a healing service* unable to speak!

Thursday night, the opening night for our meetings, finally arrived. All during the praise and worship period, I couldn't speak a word, or sing. Finally, I was introduced to the people, walked out to the podium, picked up the microphone to pray, *and suddenly* my voice boomed out in prayer *strong and loud*. This was God's dramatic victory over Satan's final attack. Glory to God! He had just manifested a Gift of Healing, and it was *for me*. Now we'll see why Satan was so desperate to stop these meetings.

After my voice supernaturally returned the moment I *started* praying, everything else seemed to click into order. Following prayer, I read two foundation scriptures and we worshipped in song a little longer than usual. I then began ministering the Word of God. At the conclusion of the message, I had not received anything from the Holy Spirit to minister to the people through His Gifts.

The music started playing, but I just stood there *not knowing what to do*. Perhaps thirty seconds passed and *I still* didn't know what to do. Then I heard my wife speak to me from about twenty feet away saying, "Call it out!" In a slightly louder frustrated voice I responded, "Call it out? Call *what* out!" She walked over to me and gave me a sheet of paper where she had written down about fifteen things the Holy Spirit had revealed to her during the service. Together we then disclosed what the Holy Spirit had revealed to her concerning the needs of the people.

The information given was totally accurate, the people responded, and signs and wonders were manifested with prayer and healings. Out of a crowd of approximately one hundred and thirty or forty people, about ten came forth to give their lives to the Lord Jesus Christ.

At the service on Friday night all things went well. The crowd was a little larger, the Gifts of the Spirit manifested in greater number and variety, and ten to twelve more people also received eternal salvation. However, a problem was emerging. The weather began to change and heavy rain was forecasted to occur on Saturday and *Saturday night*. I said to the Lord, "Lord, You know tomorrow night is the last night of our services. It's supposed to rain real heavy. If it rains, people are going to stay home. Besides that, the roof leaks really bad. There'll be water all over the floor; people will get wet, and it'll be a real problem. Lord, *please*, I don't care if it snows! Please, *please*, just don't let it rain."

Saturday night, the final night for our services, arrived. Earlier that afternoon a *few light flakes* of snow fell for a *very short* period of time. And that was all. It was remarkable! Now, all I know is that I made a serious plea to the Lord. Either the weather man was way off, or the Lord intervened into the laws of nature on our behalf. One thing is for sure; *it didn't rain!*

The service was scheduled to begin at 7:00 P.M. We arrived at the auditorium about 6:00 P.M. This allowed more time for me to pray before the service. Large numbers of people began filing in about 6:30 PM. All of the seats were taken early and extra chairs had to be brought in. The music was splendid and the atmosphere was electrifying with great excitement and expectation.

Several guest ministers were present and also the Apostle who helped to make our meetings possible. At 7:00 PM sharp, the person conducting the service welcomed everyone, acknowledged the visiting ministers, and then with the Minister of Music, led the people into singing *praises* unto the Lord. I noticed that the quality of praise was at a higher level. After the praise session was completed, a few comments were made about the previous nights' services. Some remarks were made about our ministry then my wife and I were introduced to the people. Two foundation scriptures were read and everyone entered into a phase of *worship* and singing that lasted about fifteen minutes.

As I walked to the podium, the atmosphere was so electrifying that I prayed and led the people into more worship myself. After *this* period of worship, the ministry of the Word of God began and lasted about forty-five minutes. Then we went back into *worship* again, and the Holy Spirit began to minister in full force in an environment of music that was holy, elevating, and beautiful.

The Holy Spirit enabled me to complement the numerous Gifts of the Spirit that manifested with great variation and preciseness through my wife. Magnificent signs and wonders were demonstrated by the Holy Spirit for about forty-five minutes. We later discovered that two miracles occurred without our knowledge by the sovereign ministry of the Holy Spirit Himself. One lady who had been deaf in one ear for thirty-two years received hearing in that ear. Another lady, whose big toe on one foot had turned black from diabetes, saw her toe miraculously turn from black to normal color. These were Gifts of Healings.

After ministering with the Gifts of the Holy Spirit had finished, a healing line was formed for people who were not personally ministered to by the Holy Spirit through His Gifts. The healing line was for people who wanted us to lay hands upon them to receive their healing by faith. All of the people were engaged in a very high level of *worship.* The music was gentle and glorious with the theme of Alleluia masterfully played and sung in the background. Many had their hands lifted up in total adoration of the Lord with tears running down their cheeks. Others simply had their eyes closed swaying with uplifted hands.

As we approached the healing line, it appeared to me as though we were entering into a zone of holiness. When we began to walk the healing line my wife put her hand on my back. I could feel heat and the anointing from her hand flowing through me. Then something completely unexpected, happened. As we *approached* the people in the healing line, before I could even touch them, many of them fell to the floor like falling stacked dominoes. Those who didn't fall staggered under the mighty anointing of the Holy Spirit.

After ministering healing to the people by faith, as is our practice, we told *everyone* to check with their physician to verify their healing. Next we gave an altar call and about twenty people, out of approximately three hundred present, came forth to receive the greatest of all miracles: eternal life through Christ Jesus.

What a service! I wish you were there. It highly revealed and glorified the Lord Jesus Christ, powerfully demonstrated the Kingdom of God, and magnificently blessed the people. Following the service, the Apostle who was so very helpful to us, invited us to minister at two of his churches the next day, which was Sunday. This was a wonderful surprise that we graciously accepted.

Sunday was one of those gorgeous days characteristic of the Northeast in the Fall. The air was crisp, and trees were arrayed in their entire splendor by a spectrum of red, yellow, orange, and brown leaves. The glistening gold sun was surrounded by a canapé of magnificent blue sky with a few large white clouds gently floating by. It was a gorgeous scene that only God could create, and it greeted us after a night of glorious ministry.

We crossed the Hudson River and arrived at the Apostle's New York church shortly before the 11:00 A.M. service. The Apostle introduced my wife and me as guest ministers and gave an account of what he had witnessed through our ministry at the previous night's service. The congregation received us with affection. Following the praise and worship ministry, prayer, and the reading of scripture, I then ministered the Word of God. Following the ministry of the Word, the ministry of the Holy Spirit began. Many were blessed by the Gifts of the Spirit with healing, and a few were blessed with words of comfort and encouragement. However, no one came forward to receive salvation as I recall.

The afternoon service at the Apostle's home church began at 3:00 P.M. The sanctuary was practically full with probably about five to six hundred Believers. The music was wonderful, the Word of God was rich, and the ministry of the Holy Spirit was splendid. The people were blessed, as was our team which was in attendance. Now I want to tell you something which drives home the accuracy of details that the Word of Knowledge can give.

Remember my telling you about a Word of Knowledge given to me during prayer *before* our trip occurred that showed the inside of a Jewish Temple? Well, when we arrived at the Apostle's home church we entered into a large gray stone building through a back door. He led us past a large, clean kitchen adjacent to a huge dining room with tables covered with white tablecloths. Then, we went down a broad hallway to a door that opened into the sanctuary. We entered into the sanctuary and there it was! I saw the exact magnificent Jewish sanctuary shown to me by the Holy Spirit through the Word of Knowledge weeks before I arrived there.

I beheld the white alabaster walls forming a large interior circle. The dark mahogany-looking pews had long cushions matching the beautiful blood-red carpet. But most of all, it was the domed-shaped ceiling with the magnificent Star of David in the center, that gave the sanctuary its splendor as the evening sun rays beamed through the mosaic-cut glass in colors of red, blue, yellow, and an assortment of other colors. This church building was a *former* Jewish temple.

We returned home full of joy and thanksgiving because of what the Lord had done. The Holy Spirit manifested Himself far greater than what we could have imagined. He glorified Jesus, demonstrated the Kingdom of God, proved to be a tremendous blessing to so many people, caused people to come to Christ Jesus for eternal salvation, and met our needs also.

Do you also remember my telling you about the symbolic Word of Wisdom I received during prayer while preparing for this assignment? The one depicting me coming up out of snake-infested water onto dry land with boots covering my feet and extending up beyond the water to my knees? Well, three or four weeks after we had returned home, the Holy Spirit gave me the meaning of that *symbolic* vision. When the vision occurred I had neither the time to do a word search to determine what the vision meant, nor did I have the *spiritual insight* to understand it. So it was the Holy Spirit Himself, who gave me the understanding later. Recently, I did a word study which confirmed exactly what the Holy Spirit revealed to me about that vision.

Water represents life, the Word of God, the Holy Spirit, and people. Snakes represent satanic power, demonic spirits, and evil influence. Boots represent protection, and the ability, preparation, and readiness to face the enemy with the Gospel of peace which is the Word of God, and the sword of the Spirit, and the Power of God unto salvation. Need I say more!

It wasn't until after the mission was completed, that the Holy Spirit simply revealed to me *that the vision meant* I would be among the people speaking the Word of God, be protected from all evil, and that I would come forth victoriously. Let me ask you a question. If I had known the outcome in advance, would I have prayed so fervently? Would I have depended so strongly upon the Lord? Would my faith have been tested, and then strengthened like steel?

The Holy Spirit knows what to reveal, when to reveal it, and why. I'm content to trust His judgment. For *any* assignment He may give to you, *you too* can trust Him, and His Gifts!

CHAPTER SEVENTEEN

THE FLORIDA ASSIGNMENT

Aside from similar directions from the Holy Spirit, the overwhelming difference between the New Jersey assignment and *this* assignment is that the New Jersey assignment was a trip to minister, as a *Minister*, to Christians and others *in a public setting*. The Florida assignment on the other hand, was a trip to minister as a *regular Believer*, just as you may be, to an *individual person in a private setting*.

But *the most important thing* the Holy Spirit wants us to realize is the vast love God has for those whom He has created, and the length that He will go to help *anyone*. When people continually reject the Lord Jesus Christ as their personal Savior, God is still an everlasting, loving God who provides numerous opportunities for them to come to Him through Christ Jesus; even in very difficult circumstances.

Once again it was during Springtime that this assignment began. One year after the New Jersey assignment, the Holy Spirit spoke to me early in the morning and directed me to go to the local medical school library. I was to check out the Help Wanted section in the Journal of the American Dental Association. I arrived at the library about 9:30 A.M., obtained the journal, and surveyed the states where I was licensed to practice. My eyes fell upon an advertisement seeking a general dentist to work at a clinic located in a small city north of Tampa, in Florida.

The advertisement was a request for help placed by a long time professional friend of mine who was a superb oral surgeon. I use to refer patients to him when I practiced in South Miami. I called him about the advertisement and this was his response: "Gene Givens, I can't believe it. I was just thinking about you two days ago, wondering where you were and what you are doing." Following some small talk, he told me about their clinic, personnel need, and asked me to come down and help. I told him I would get back to him the next day.

After spending considerable time with the Lord complaining, moaning, groaning, and giving all kinds of reasons why I shouldn't leave my family, my wife convinced me that just maybe the Lord *wanted* me to go. Later, I went back to the Lord and let Him know that I wasn't overly enthused about going to Florida. But I made it clear however, that if that was what He wanted me to do, I would go. As promised I called my friend the next day, and accepted his offer.

Several days later, I was on the way to Florida. After driving about three hours, the Holy Spirit spoke to me very, very clearly. He said, "Something catastrophic is going to happen to one of their children!" That was a Word of Wisdom, and it was somewhat mystifying. It involved something God thoroughly knew about that was going to happen in the future. I didn't understand *what* He meant. A child, something is going to happen to a child? All I knew was that in some kind of way it was connected with my trip.

After arriving in Florida, I went directly to the clinic to meet the friend I hadn't seen in over twenty years. We had a great reunion, and he showed a lot of curiosity about my being a minister. He also expressed wonderment that another dentist he was going to interview the next day was also a minister. After receiving some clinic orientation I left to find a place to stay.

Three weeks later I decided to spend the weekend with a friend and his wife in Lakeland. We had a wonderful weekend together and we all decided it would be better for me to go back to the clinic early Monday morning instead of driving such a long distance Sunday night.

Leaving early Monday morning, I arrived to the clinic at 8:30 A.M. and found everybody in utter chaos. I buttonholed one the assistants to find out what in the world was going on. "Haven't you heard, haven't you heard? It's been all over the TV and radio!" Then she told me the terrible story. On Sunday, my friend's daughter was in a horrific auto accident and thrown from a jeep she was riding in. She was transferred to a major trauma care hospital in Tampa, *but was not expected to live.*

Suddenly, *everything* became instantly clear to me. I knew exactly why the Lord sent me there, and I knew exactly what to do! I recalled the Word of Wisdom given to me, "Something catastrophic is going to happen to one of their children." The child was my friend's young adult-daughter. This caused my faith once again to be hardened like steel. Following the work day, I went to the hospital late that night.

Fortunately, I carried my ministry license and ordination papers which enabled me to be allowed into the intensive care area. I deliberately sought access late at night in hopes of avoiding visitors. The hospital was about an hour and fifteen minutes away. On the way there, I recall talking to the Lord about the difficulty I may encounter ministering to the daughter of my friend in the intensive care area where other patients and staff may be. I arrived at the hospital about 10:30 P.M. and was given permission for access to the Intensive Care Unit. God had prepared *everything* in advance!

My friend's daughter had been placed in a *private* ICU room with seemingly thick walls and a door all by herself. Her father was there with her, alone. He came over, hugged me, and said, "Gene, all I know is, this is why you're here." He then told me what had happened to his daughter, explained that they had obtained the very *best of the best* surgeons who operated on her, but was told by them that there *was no way she could survive.* Then he left, closed the door, and I was left alone with her.

His daughter was lying there, head bandaged from brain surgery, faced partially bandaged, tremendously bloated and swollen, tubes down her nose and throat, connected to intravenous bags, monitors, and she was extremely pale. By the power of the Holy Spirit and in the Name of the Lord Jesus Christ, the first things I did were to bind an evil spirit that could take her life, and speak to her condition to declare that she would live and not die. For the next hour I laid my hands on her and prayed with my understanding and in the Spirit.

This I did almost nightly for three weeks. At times my friend, the other dentist who also was a minister, and I would pray over her together. Her condition didn't seem to physically improve, but the doctors were *astounded* that she was *still* alive.

Then one night the Lord gave me a Word of Wisdom in a vision. In the vision, I saw the owner of the clinic and his wife, wearing an unusual looking dress, come into the clinic and tell me to leave. The next morning the vision came to pass, in precise detail, *exactly* as it was shown to me. On occasions, I would pray with "their" patients in "their" clinic. This was considered inappropriate.

After returning to my apartment to pack for my return trip home, I decided to visit my friend. His daughter was still unconscious. He welcomed me with graciousness, thanked me for ministering to his daughter, and told me he was aware of what happened at the clinic. Then, he made a very unusual remark. He said, "I knew you had to see me before you left to finish things up with me." We both knew he wasn't referring to anything professionally, *but spiritually*.

Knowing that he was Jewish, I gently and carefully explained to him the plan of salvation through Jesus Christ beginning with the Old Testament and culminating with the New Testament. I then explained to him the process of being born again. With total sincerity he said, "Gene, I really appreciate this, but I am Jewish." We parted ways with me knowing that he still had a very special place in the heart of God and that he is deeply loved by God; as the phenomenal blessing that he and his daughter later received, proves. Being a Believer or not, he remains one of the finest professionals I've had the privilege of knowing and really like.

Back home a week or so later, my wife called me to the telephone. My friend from Florida was calling me. Initially my heart sank little bit until I heard the tone of his voice and his remarks. He informed me that his precious daughter *woke up, and was in her perfect mind!*

The Holy Spirit may not use you exactly in *this* manner, but there are people you can touch for God that nobody else can. Be open for Him to use you to help others in special ways. In the process you will glorify the Lord Jesus Christ, demonstrate the love and power of the Kingdom of God, and be a blessing to them. Some may even desire to have *what you have*. Offer them Jesus Christ.

The Word of God tells us that we are God's workmanship created in Christ Jesus *for good works* that God has *already prepared* for us to walk in. These two assignments certainly verify this scripture. The works that were accomplished were good, and the Holy Spirit led us on the paths to accomplish them. God has paths for you to walk, too. All that's required is to receive Jesus Christ as your personal Savior, and allow the Holy Spirit to lead you and work through you.[1]

Supporting Scriptures
Florida Assignment
Please read the scriptures

---

[1] Eph 2:10, Ps 32:8, Rom 8:14

CHAPTER EIGHTEEN

THE SECRET OF WORSHIP

Worship is so essential, and so much related to the Holy Spirit and His Gifts, that I elevate *this subject* to the highest level. Just as Jesus Christ is the Master *connection* between the Holy Spirit, His Gifts, and His Power, love is the Master *attribute* between the Holy Spirit, His Gifts, and His Power. And the way *we demonstrate* that love is through worship to God.

The secret of worship is that we experience the presence of God, *and His reaction to us* due to our worshipping Him![A] Worship is ministering to God. God is love. We worship God by expressing our warm, personal affection, devotion, and adoration of Him, *to Him*. In worship we *tell Him* how much we esteem Him, treasure Him, and cherish Him. By worship *we demonstrate* how much we idolize Him, adore Him, and exalt Him. It is through worship that we fulfill the first and greatest *commandment* of God given to us from Jesus Christ: to love the Lord our God with all of our heart, and with all of our soul, and with all of our strength, and with all of our mind.

Worship our Father who is the Lord God Almighty, worship the Lord Jesus Christ, and worship the Holy Spirit.[1] In the process we experience intimate relationships based

---

[A] **See page 203, paragraph 3, and page 204, paragraphs 1 and 2.**

upon heartfelt love and adoration. During worship, the Holy Spirit can literally elevate our spirit into the discernable presence of God. This alone makes worship the most premier experience we can have with God; for we can find ourselves in the presence of Love, in an atmosphere of peace that truly does pass all understanding, and in a secret place where the Gifts of the Spirit can flow unhindered.

Angels worship Jesus, demons worshipped Jesus, and just like the Levites, elders of old, and heavenly angelic beings, we too will be among the multitudes who shall worship Him in heaven and throughout all of eternity.[2] No other endeavor touches His heart to respond on our behalf like worship does. And, quite often God responds to worship with the Gifts of the Holy Spirit, or directions from the Holy Spirit.[3] We worship God in our own private settings, in public corporate settings, and in services that we provide for Him to others. I have experienced the Gifts of the Spirit in operation in all of these types of settings. You can have these experiences too.

Worship and Music

Worship is greatly enhanced in an atmosphere of soft, beautiful music and periods of reverent silence. As symbolized, the Holy Spirit is extremely gentle and as sensitive as a dove. The fire of His power, like we see with the Gift of Faith, the Working of Miracles, or the Gifts of Healings, is reserved for His activities in destroying the works of the devil. But His other Gifts often manifest while we are basking in the glory of His Presence with soft, beautiful, and holy music playing as we commune with Him, and worship Him.

The Key to Corporate Worship with Music

The key to corporate worship with music lies with church Leadership. I'm talking about the minister in charge of conducting the service, and the minister in charge of conducting the *music for worship*. The quality and level of worship obtained in corporate settings is directly related to the amount of time, quality, and the level of worship experienced by Leadership, especially the Music Minister, during their times of *personal worship*. True worship can never be practiced for performance. It must flow from the heart by the Holy Spirit. According to John 4:23, in the Contemporary English version of the Bible, Jesus Himself said, "But a time is coming, and it is already here! Even now the true worshipers are being led by the Spirit to worship the Father according to the truth. These are the ones the Father is seeking to worship Him." Now let me give you two contrasting results to worship in actual services that I attended.

A number of years ago my wife and I joined a fellowship that held services in a tent, then moved into a vacant used car building as late Fall approached. The Pastor and his wife were truly Christ-centered. They were spiritually mature and realized the importance of having Five Fold Ministry Gifts offered through various apostles, prophets, evangelists, pastors and teachers to visit and help them to build up the congregation for the work of the ministry. Thus, they were faithful in doing what scripture says to do.

One Sunday evening, a visiting minister was to bring the message and minister to the congregation. After a time of praise, the Music Minister led the congregation into a high level of worship *with* music that transitioned into singing in the Spirit *without* music. As though on cue, the Holy Spirit led all Believers to stop all singing and a period of total silence ensued. Then the Holy Presence of the Lord became discernible. In quietness, the minister gently asked the congregation, "Do you smell that?"

A glorious fragrance flowed throughout the congregation with a smell far more wonderful than that of a gardenia. This was the manifestation of one of the Gifts of the Holy Spirit called the Discerning of spirits. Thus, some of us were enabled to smell the sweet savors of our worship going up before God. The Holy Spirit was actually revealing what scripture says happens when we pray.[4] Worship is a type of prayer. That entire worship experience was marvelous. Here we also see an excellent example of mature Leadership who knew how to flow with the ministry of the Holy Spirit in worship. Now let's look at another real life example where someone innocently quenched the Holy Spirit during worship *before* He could complete His ministry. You will notice a very different result.

During services at a different church, we noticed how the Minister of Music also brought the congregation up to a very high level of worship with soft beautiful music. Some people were whispering words of adulation to God, others were gently sobbing with tears, while many were simply basking in the Presence of the Lord.

Then suddenly, the entire mood of the congregation was disrupted as someone began clapping hands loudly and hollering out praises to God. The Presence of the Holy Spirit left! The mood of worship collapsed, and the congregation seemed to be let down like a high flying balloon that suddenly lost all of its air. There's a place for mighty praise. But praise should never be mixed up and intermingled with worship. Worship and praise are two different kinds of prayer used for different purposes at *different times*.

Again, the Holy Spirit is extremely gentle and sensitive like the dove that He symbolizes. The least unexpected noise or disorder causes Him to fly away. Emotional hype and generated excitement *is not worship.*

If you are in a Leadership position in the church, spend time in worshipping God personally, alone. Ask the Holy Spirit to teach you His gentle ways, and how to follow Him in worship. Be prepared for a glorious experience.

Supporting Scriptures:
Worship
Please read the scriptures

---

[1] Ezec 46:3, 1 Sam 3:1, Jn 4:23, 24, Ps 95:6, 103:1, 104:1, 29:2, 86:9

[2] Heb 1:6, Mk 5:1-6, Neh 9:5-6, Rev 4:10, 11, 7:9-11

[3] Mt 2:1, 2, 8:2, 3, 9:18, 19, Acts 13:2

[4] Rev 8:3, 4, Ps 141:2

CHAPTER NINETEEN

ESSENTIAL STEPS TO TAKE

Since we now have a good understanding of the Holy Spirit, His Gifts, and His Power, this chapter is included to assist us in putting ourselves into a better position to enable these monumental blessings to become operative in our lives. We'll structure this information *as steps to take, additional foundations, and activities to pursue*. All or part of this information is applicable to everyone; from the unbeliever, to the new Believer, to the mature Believer. This information is intended to help us all move up higher in God. I hope you will find it to be very useful. Here is the first step to take.

Obtain Eternal Salvation

The Holy Spirit is *available* for *everyone*. His Gifts are available *to all Believers* according *to His will*. The Holy Spirit is the One who executes all of the activities of God for those who are in the Kingdom of God and on behalf of those who *want to be in* the Kingdom of God. However, the *only* way to receive the Holy Spirit, His Gifts and His Power, is to *first* receive the Lord Jesus Christ as your personal Savior. *This is the first essential step to take.* Everything that enables *this* to happen is a function of the Holy Spirit also.

How to Obtain Eternal Salvation

So how does one obtain eternal salvation? It is so simple that Satan *deceives* people by making it seem like a fairy tale and therefore *silly, unnecessary*, and *hard to believe*. It is simply a matter of *believing* the Gospel of Jesus Christ *by faith* and *confessing* that you believe it with your mouth. You're not required to prove it. You're not required to analyze it. You're not even required to understand it! You don't have to go to a church. You don't have to go to a priest. You don't have to go through some kind of ceremony. You don't have to go through any kind of hoops or loops. All you have to do is *what the Word of God* ***in the Holy Bible*** *tells you to do*. And that is to, *by faith*, believe the Gospel with all of your heart and *confess* that you believe it with your mouth. Scripture itself tells us not to be deceived from the simplicity of Christ.[1] Jesus Christ is *the only* way to God the Father. He was crucified on the cross, He was buried, He was resurrected from the dead, and He shall come again to judge both the living and the dead.[2]

Here is how *scripture defines* the simple truth of the Gospel: Christ died for our sins according to the scriptures. He was buried. He rose again the third day according to the scriptures.[3] According to *scripture* this is how you receive eternal salvation through Christ Jesus: *Confess* with your mouth the Lord Jesus, believe that He died and was buried, and *believe* with your heart that God has raised Jesus from the dead. *This is step one. You* can do this *right now wherever* you are! It's done through prayer, and now we're going to see how to pray for this eternal blessing.

The Prayer for Eternal Salvation

Here is the prayer to *believe* and *confess* with your mouth to God in order to receive Jesus Christ as your personal Savior.

"God Almighty, I call on the Name of the Lord Jesus Christ to be saved. Jesus, I believe You died for my sins according to the scriptures. I believe that You were buried. I believe God raised You from the dead the third day according to the scriptures. I receive You as my personal Savior right now."

That's it! If you really believe in your heart the prayer you just confessed to God, you *now* have right standing with God and you are now saved. *Scripture* tells us *why* this is true. It is true because:

"With the heart man believeth unto righteousness; and with the mouth confession is made unto salvation. Whosoever shall call upon the Name of the Lord shall be saved."

Upon receiving the Lord Jesus Christ as your personal Savior, you instantly undergo a *spiritual* change. Your mind is the same; it *must* be renewed by the Word of God and perfected by the Holy Spirit. Your body is the same; you don't look any older, you don't look any younger, you normally look the same. However, the Holy Spirit sometimes causes a Heavenly glow to be on the face of a new Believer that people can recognize. But if you're sick, your body can be healed by faith or by the Gifts of the Holy Spirit.[4] You may, or may not *feel* the same, although some people sense a certain type of joy. The process of salvation is *independent of feelings*, but *totally dependent* upon compliance with the Word of God.

But salvation is merely *the beginning!* If you have taken this step for the first time, there is something else you must do. You must grow in this new found life of a Believer by diligently seeking to receive the Baptism with the Holy Spirit, and seeking the Kingdom of God and His righteousness.[5] Pray sincerely, diligently, and ask the Holy Spirit to guide you to the church or fellowship where you will be nurtured with sound Biblical doctrine, built up on the Word of God, and groomed for the destiny God has available for you here upon Earth and in the Kingdom of God. Sound Bible doctrine *must* include: the reality of hell, Heaven, and eternal salvation through Christ Jesus. The Person, works, present-day Ministry of the Lord Jesus Christ *and* the Holy Spirit. The New Covenant, the return of the Lord Jesus Christ, prophetic events fulfilled and those *yet to be* fulfilled. And, God's plan for mankind's eternal destiny. Being shepherded by a Christ-centered pastor who embraces the Holy Spirit, His Gifts, power, and the commandments of Jesus Christ will be a major blessing to you. Pray diligently to find such a pastor. Now, here is the second essential step to take.

Obtain the Baptism with the Holy Spirit

Obtaining the Baptism with the Holy Spirit is the most important event any Believer can experience *after* receiving salvation through Christ Jesus. Since we are discussing the Holy Spirit, His Gifts, and His power, it would be unforgivable not to carefully examine the Baptism with the Holy Spirit and His supernatural expression called "speaking in tongues".

There is a level of understanding for everybody. God knows this! Jesus knows this, and so did the Apostle Paul. Both Jesus and Paul told their followers, in essence, that there were certain spiritual things they couldn't be told because they weren't ready to hear it. There were things too deep and too heavy for them to understand and receive until the Holy Spirit arrived to guide them into all truth.[6]

God has always revealed His knowledge and His doctrines line upon line, precept upon precept, here a little and there a little.[7] He does the same thing today through His Word and by the Holy Spirit! Because of the times in which we are living, His Word is being revealed to us in an accelerated manner. Following eternal salvation through the Lord Jesus Christ, excluding worship, the Baptism with the Holy Spirit and speaking in tongues are the most important spiritual experiences available to any Believer. Therefore, given the extensive amount of misinformation, confusion, and marginalization about these two experiences, this is another good time to pray and ask the Holy Spirit to reveal what He wants you to receive regarding the following *scriptural* presentation about these two most vital subjects.

About the Baptism with the Holy Spirit

The Baptism with the Holy Spirit is *a commandment* given by Jesus Christ Himself, through the Holy Spirit, and it is recorded in scripture. [8] It is a Divine instruction that applies to all Believers.

The word commandment in this context means to order, enjoin or give a charge as a military commander instructs his troops. This manner of commandment was given by Jesus Christ regarding His charge for "The Great Commission," and was given by God, and by Moses.

Therefore, *the reasons* for such instructions must be extremely important because the instructions came from the very highest levels of authority. [9]

No serious student of God's Word would argue that "The Great Commission" given by Jesus Christ to go into all of the world, preach the Gospel, and make disciples, were instructions *limited* to His Apostles. This same "Commission" still applies to Believers today. [10]

Therefore, it's only logical that the commandment Jesus gave to His Apostles, by the Holy Spirit, to wait and be baptized with power, meaning the Holy Spirit, was also not limited to His Apostles. But, like "The Great Commission," it too would apply to Believers today. This truth is established throughout the Book of the Acts, the Book of First Corinthians, and is demonstrated by many Believers today. For clearer understanding, please read the Supporting Scriptures referenced here and those listed under references 9 and 10 above. [11]

In the very first chapter of the Book of the Acts of the Apostles, this commandment is revealed and its purpose is clearly stated by Jesus Himself. Jesus told His disciples to wait for the promise of the Father which they had heard of from Him. He told them that the Prophet John baptized with water but that they would be baptized with the Holy Ghost, and receive power so that they could be witnesses for Him. There are two important things for us to notice here. First, water is a substance whereas the Holy Spirit is a Divine Person. There's a big difference between being baptized with *a physical substance* as a symbol for an inward change, compared to being baptized with a Divine Being who has power to help us for the kind of work necessary to be a witness for Jesus Christ.

Secondly, notice also that this commandment occurred at the end of forty days just before Jesus was taken up into Heaven. The subject He talked about during those forty days is so important that it is actually revealed in scripture. He talked about *things pertaining to the Kingdom of God!* We know from scripture that the Holy Spirit and His power are inseparable from activities demonstrated and associated with the Kingdom of God. **Therefore, it seems clear that the purpose of the commandment is to insure that the Believer has the *indwelling* of the Holy Spirit with power, to enable that Believer to be a powerful witness and operative *with* the Lord Jesus Christ to demonstrate the Kingdom of God on earth.** [12]

The Baptism with the Holy Spirit is necessary to have the power to be an effective witness to carry out the works of Jesus Christ, and for effective ministry. Scripture reveals that Jesus linked being a witness *with* the Holy Ghost and power. [13] The Apostle Paul stated that his preaching was in demonstration of the Spirit and power.

Don't Be Confused

Given the confusion and misunderstanding surrounding the Baptism with the Holy Spirit, it is necessary to show that this commandment was not limited or intended *only for the Apostles* of the Early Church, but *extends to all Believers* throughout this Dispensation of Grace in which we are living. In addition, let's allow scripture to verify *the sign* that accompany and confirm the Baptism with the Holy Spirit in a Believer.

It is clearly *established in scripture* that the Baptism with the Holy Spirit has a definite sign, manifestation, or *evidence displayed by the Believer* in whom the baptism has occurred. The baptism and its evidence were prophesied in the Old Testament, by John the Baptist, and by Jesus Himself. It was demonstrated in the Early Church. It is promised to all who called upon the Name of the Lord. *The evidence of the Baptism with the Holy Spirit is speaking in tongues.*[14]

Scripture tells us *to ask* for this experience.[15] The Holy Spirit's *indwelling* usually does not automatically occur when we receive Jesus Christ as our personal Savior. Jesus clearly tells us that the Father gives the Holy Spirit to them *that ask Him*. If receiving the Baptism with the Holy Spirit *was automatic* with receiving Jesus as Savior, He would not have instructed us to ask for this experience. But we do have the Holy Spirit *with us* from that moment we receive Jesus as Savior. The *indwelling* of the Holy Spirit is an altogether different experience, evidenced by speaking with tongues, available *after* salvation through Christ Jesus has occurred. Here's a scriptural example of this truth.

The Apostle Paul encountered a group of disciples in a city called Ephesus. He asked them if they had received the Holy Ghost *since* they *believed.* They didn't know who the Holy Spirit was! In fact they said, "We have not so much heard whether there be any Holy Ghost." Upon further questioning they told Paul that they were baptized by John the Baptist *to believe* on Jesus Christ. So these were *saved* disciples. Paul then laid his hands upon them, the Holy Ghost came upon them and they *spoke in tongues*. The Holy Spirit then even manifested the Gift of Prophecy through them![16]

The Baptism with the Holy Spirit is what John the Baptist meant when he said Jesus would baptize us with the Holy Ghost and fire. It is what Jesus meant when He said, "Out of your belly shall flow rivers of living water." It is also what Jesus meant when He said, *"Those who believe"* would be those who were baptized, believed the gospel, *and who would speak with new tongues*.[17] This experience can be received as a result of personal prayer or through the laying on of hands by other Believers empowered with the Holy Spirit.

How to Obtain the Baptism with the Holy Spirit

The commandments of the Lord are not oppressive, burdensome, nor grievous. The Lord would not require us to do something that we were incapable of doing. Receiving the Baptism with the Holy Spirit is *a promise* given by God the Father Himself. Furthermore it is Jesus Christ who baptizes us with the Holy Spirit and fire, and who told us that if we asked the Father anything in His Name, *He* would do it. We have not, because *we ask not*. But we must have the right motive and purpose for asking to receive. We can obtain the Baptism with the Holy Spirit by prayer.

Prayer to Receive the Baptism with the Holy Spirit

To receive the Baptism with the Holy Spirit, all a Believer has to do is to pray to the Father, in the Name of the Lord Jesus Christ, and ask to be baptized with the Holy Spirit and power. Here's how it is done.

"Father,

In accordance with Your promise, and the commandment of Jesus Christ, I ask to be baptized with the Holy Spirit and power. I receive Him now with thanksgiving.

In the Name of the Lord Jesus Christ I pray,

Amen."

This is obeying Jesus' own commandment. Jesus said if we knew "how to give good gifts to our own children, *how much more* shall our Heavenly Father give the Holy Spirit to them that ask Him!" Therefore expect to receive the promise by faith and continually thank God until the promise occurs. The Holy Spirit will use your tongue to make utterances you do not understand. This is proof of your baptism with the Holy Spirit.

God gives us *free will* to choose to obey this commandment and obtain this blessed experience, or not to. But as previously stated, it is available to as many who call upon the Name of Jesus Christ for salvation.

The Value of Speaking in Tongues

Since speaking in tongues is the sign of having been baptized with the Holy Spirit, we need to take a closer look *at this* supernatural phenomenon.

Speaking in tongues is so valuable that a considerable amount of scripture is allocated to the subject. As is true with any other subject, *scripture* from the Word of God *must* be our final authority when it comes to speaking in tongues; not *our* opinion, traditions, or personal belief. God is not going to change. Nor is His Word going to change. It is we who must change to accept His Word rather than ignore His Word if it conflicts with our personal opinion or belief. So let's see what His Word has to say about this experience called "speaking in tongues."

We discover from the scriptures that speaking in tongues is a supernatural manifestation resulting from the Baptism with the Holy Spirit.[18] Tongues can be in a language unknown to the speaker but known to the hearers, or in a language unknown to either.[19] Tongues also involve two of the Divine Vocal Communication Gifts of the Spirit.[20] Most significantly, it is ordained by God for the Church and is listed along with apostles, teachers, helps, governments, and other essential components of the New Testament church.[21] Despite this, there were those in the Early Church era, and there are those today, who still do not speak in tongues. However, it is instructional to note that the Apostle Paul said, "I would that ye *all* spoke in tongues."[22]

Other Uses for Tongues

The supernatural manifestation of tongues is given to Believers to aid them in their individual prayer life, worship, and praise to God. When the Holy Spirit intercedes through you in this fashion, it is always according to the *will of God* for the *person* or *situation* the Spirit is interceding through you for. This occurs in a language the speaker *does not* understand.

It is the Holy Spirit who gives these manifestations, but the will to cooperate with Him to enable them to occur is under the control of the Believer. Praying in tongues is extremely beneficial when you have exhausted your ability to pray with your normal understanding or when you don't know how to pray as you ought to.[23] This is called *praying in the Spirit*. The Apostle Paul stated that he prayed in the spirit *and* prayed with his understanding.[24] He also stated that he spoke in tongues more than the rest and he gave a strong warning to the church that speaking in tongues *should not* be forbidden.[25]

If you desire to speak in tongues or operate with the Gifts of the Spirit you desire good things ordained by God. He provides plenty of scriptural proof of others who did so in the Early Church, just as there are many who also do so today. There are a great number of scriptures *that support* speaking in tongues, but there are *none* that discourage this experience. Any resistance to these experiences is man-made *and* is not scriptural.

The Comfort of a Personal Experience

Sometimes when you are being introduced to the spiritual reality of a scriptural doctrine that you are unfamiliar with, or have little knowledge about, there's a natural tendency to be somewhat hesitant to accept it. Actually, that's a good way to be until there is sufficient time for the Holy Spirit to confirm to you *from the scriptures* the significance and truth of the subject. But God is the God of all comfort and the Holy Spirit is the Comforter who will not lead you astray.[26] He knows and fully understands the extent and depth of spiritual knowledge that all of us have. He wants us to have more, but He also knows our hesitancy when it comes to our willingness to accept a spiritual truth that we are unfamiliar with, or to be blunt and honest, somewhat leery about. Because I was like this, I perceive that the Holy Spirit would have me share with you the experience I had about speaking in tongues and the way I was heartened. Hopefully, my experience will be of value and encouragement to you if you are still cautious about speaking in tongues.

God has a way of putting people into our lives and creating circumstances to get us where He wants us to be and to accomplish that which concerns us *for His purpose*. Such was the case with me when our oldest son elected to paint a very small *main-line* denominational church building in New York as his Eagle Scout project. During a work session, I had the opportunity of meeting the church Pastor. He had an extremely gentle spirit and was very low key. As a southerner, his southern denomination made an excellent choice in selecting him to serve in such a high strung, impatient, cosmopolitan area.

When he discovered that I was a professor in the School of Dentistry at the Medical Center, he informed me that he held Bible studies there once a week and invited me to attend. *Believe me, at that time, this was the last thing I ever wanted to do!* But out of courtesy, I agreed.

One day during the lunch period, while walking down the hallway with several *students*, I encountered this Pastor coming towards me. "Oh, Dr. Givens, I'm going to have a Bible study right now. Why don't you join us?" Caught! No way do I want these students to see *me* going into a *Bible study*. But I had given my word to him, so I attended.

His presentation was excellent. It related to real life experiences and gave solutions based strictly upon scripture. Plus, his demeanor was gentle and he appeared knowledgeable. I had been to a lot of churches, but *this* was new to me. When I would ask an *intellectual* question designed to stump him, he would *always* answer my question with scripture that I *could not* refute. I found myself hungry for what he taught and became a diligent student. He became my confidant in spiritual things. I'm relating this as background information for an upcoming experience that involved speaking in tongues.

Several months later I received a phone call from a Christian university asking me to visit and to consider taking a position on their faculty. My professional credentials and background nicely met their needs. I went. During the visit my wife and I were required to attend a chapel service. During the service I discerned an *overwhelming* presence of God, heard people worshipping God by "singing in the Spirit," and heard "speaking in tongues" for the first time.

Hearing thousands of people singing in the Spirit without any musical background, was the most beautiful and holy sound I had ever heard. Yet, hearing individuals speaking in tongues concerned me and made me uncomfortable. I didn't know what speaking in tongues was all about, and I certainly didn't want to get myself aligned with some kind of weird religion or cult!

Upon returning home I immediately contacted the Pastor I had befriended and rehearsed everything that happened; including my awe regarding the presence of God, hearing singing in the Spirit, and my concerns about speaking in tongues. I wanted to know if speaking in tongues was of God, or something related to some kind of cult. Given this Pastor's theological knowledge, membership in a well known southern church denomination, his experience and sincerity, I felt comfortable asking his advice.

First, he assured me that what I experienced *was of God* and then *proved it* to me *by scripture*. Then he dropped a "spiritual bomb shell." He said, "Gene, I've been baptized with the Holy Spirit, and I speak in tongues. But it's not accepted by my denomination, so very few people know it." That comment eliminated all of my concerns.

There is no way I can express to you how reassuring that was to me at that particular time when I was perplexed. If you have any concerns about speaking in tongues or the Baptism with the Holy Spirit, I hope what I have shared will encourage you and eliminate all doubt.

The Baptism with the Holy Spirit Affects Two Kingdoms

One of the major benefits of the Baptism with the Holy Spirit is that it enables us to demonstrate the Kingdom of God, and also, literally overcome and dominate the kingdom of darkness according to the faith and power that is within us. Therefore, the Believer who is baptized with the Holy Spirit can have a tremendous affect in the Kingdom of God *and* on the kingdom of darkness.

You've heard about the Kingdom of God. Now is a good time to learn a few more things about it. But first we must realize that in terms of spiritual realities, the Kingdom of God and the kingdom of darkness are two very different kinds of kingdoms. We'll look at the Kingdom of God first.

The Kingdom of God

The Kingdom of God is under the Lordship of Jesus Christ. It is eternal and the people in it have eternal life with God forever. These people will always be in the "family of God," which consists of all who are in Heaven *and* those who are alive on the Earth that belong to Jesus.[27] The Kingdom of God in Heaven is literal. The Kingdom of God on Earth *now* is spiritual, but can be and is, demonstrated by Believers through the Holy Spirit. This is because, in answer to the prayer of Jesus, the Holy Spirit brings God the Father and Jesus Christ to dwell within Believers who have been baptized with the Holy Spirit. Jesus is the King; and a kingdom is wherever the king is. Therefore, as Jesus said, the Kingdom is within us.[28]

However, the Kingdom of God *will be* literal upon the Earth like it is in Heaven, when the Lord Jesus Christ returns to rule and reign on the Earth. The Kingdom of God is righteousness, and peace, and joy in the Holy Spirit.[29] The Kingdom of God is governed by God Almighty, the Lord Jesus Christ, and the Holy Spirit. The Kingdom of God includes Believers alive now on Earth, people in Heaven, the holy angels of God, and other holy beings that are in Heaven.

There are two things we should know about the Kingdom of God right *now!* First, all of the power and resources of God are resident within His Kingdom. Secondly, the Lord Jesus Christ has already revealed to us, through scripture, the nature and works related to the Kingdom of God.

By the Holy Spirit, His Power and Gifts, Jesus Christ demonstrated absolute and total power, domination and supremacy over *all* things. Therefore evil spirits, which are Satan's own forces and power, were subdued. Forces of nature were brought under control. The dead were brought back to life. All manner of sicknesses, diseases, and infirmities were healed. Civil needs were met. Basic human needs were met. Social needs were met.[30] Now, the same Lord Jesus Christ instructs His Believers to do the same works He did by the same Holy Spirit, power and spiritual Gifts.[31] Believers are to start demonstrating the Kingdom of God *now*, for eventually the *Kingdom of God* will be *given to us* to administer, under Christ, throughout all of eternity.[32] The Kingdom of God shall *never* come to an end.[33]

The Kingdom of Darkness

Now let's get some insight into the kingdom of darkness. The kingdom of darkness is also known as "this world's system." That's because it is under the spiritual control and influence of the "god of this world" who is Satan. This kingdom is the extreme opposite of the Kingdom of God. Its operatives *oppose* the Kingdom of God in every possible way they can. The kingdom of darkness *will* come to an end.

Since the spiritual fall of Adam and Eve, *everyone* born into this world is born into an *already existing condition* called sin; which is under the control of Satan. He is the author and cause of sin and he is called the prince of the powers of darkness and evil. Satan operates his kingdom by evil spirits and human beings *who know how* to operate with evil powers. Satan and his operatives have influence in greed, sickness, disease, lack, want, poverty, and world events in addition to all manner of wickedness and ungodliness. The outcome for the kingdom of darkness is eternal death.[34]

But here is the good news. Due to the finished work of Jesus Christ on the cross, Jesus, who *is the way*, has made the way for *all* people to be translated *from* the kingdom and power of darkness, and *from* the authority of Satan, and *from* the control and influence of evil powers, *into* the Kingdom of God.[35] This transfer is enabled by the Holy Spirit when one receives the Lord Jesus Christ as his or her personal Savior.

It is astounding and sad, that Satan, all evil spirits, and most of his demonic operatives *believe in* and know the reality of the Lord Jesus Christ. Yet, millions of people God has created and love, by their own choice, will *not believe in Him*![36]

Believers in the Kingdom of God have available to them special weapons that are not of a human nature. They are effective and dominate in both the *spirit realm* and this *earthly realm*. They are effective and dominate in the Kingdom of God for blessings, and in the kingdom of darkness *against* evil activities and the influence of the powers of darkness. These spiritual weapons are awesome and mighty through God. They include the Name of Jesus, the Blood of Jesus, the Word of God, prayer, the Holy Spirit and His Gifts.[37]

Once you're in the Kingdom of God and see

wonderful results from prayer, the supreme authority in the Name of Jesus Christ, and the marvelous manifestations of the Gifts of the Holy Spirit, you will know by experience the reality of the Lord Jesus Christ, the Holy Spirit, God, and the Kingdom of God.

Keys to the Kingdom of God

The depth and experiences available in the things of God are inexhaustible. But He will never take you beyond where *you* desire to go. In the process however, there are certain keys for success in *His* eyes. These keys apply to *all*, whether you are a new Believer, a long time Believer, a church leader, or a minister in the Body of Christ. Now, invite the Holy Spirit to give you some insight regarding the overview of these keys.

The Bible states that after God had revealed to the Apostle Peter that Jesus is The Christ, the Son of the Living God, Jesus then informed Peter that He would build His Church upon that revelation. He further stated that the gates of hell would not prevail against it; meaning His Church. Then Jesus did something powerful. He gave Peter the *keys* to the Kingdom of Heaven. The symbolic importance of keys is authority. When *you have* the keys you have the authority to allow yourself *and others* access into a place, and you have the authority to keep them out. The significance of what Jesus was saying is that He gives to those who know who He is, and who choose to belong to Him, keys to have access to the Kingdom of God.[38]

Jesus had access to all of the resources of Heaven to enable Him to be of *service to people* here upon the Earth. That access was through prayer and the Holy Spirit. Jesus now gives to those who belong to Him, keys for *the same* access to Heaven, to draw from the same resources, by t*he same* Holy Spirit that He had. Now, we too are to overcome evil and be of great *service to people* just as He was. God is all about people, service to people, and His Kingdom. That's why Jesus was a Servant, and why God sent the Holy Spirit with spiritual Gifts to help Him without limits. Our role is to be a servant like Jesus with the help of *the same* Holy Spirit.

There are some essential keys that the Holy Spirit has revealed to me that I will share with you. Although the Holy Spirit may reveal additional things to you, this a good place to start.

Whereas Eternal Salvation through Jesus Christ and the Baptism with the Holy Spirit are the most important steps anyone can take, there are other qualities we must possess, activities we must engage in, and scriptural facts we must accept for the Holy Spirit and His Gifts to effectively help us to demonstrate the Kingdom of God and be a blessing to people. Aside from Jesus Christ Himself, the *guiding foundation* we must embrace is love and making the Word of God our *final authority*. The *activities* we must engage in are prayer and acting by faith to demonstrate the Kingdom of God.

The Foundation of Love

The major foundation for the Gifts of the Holy Spirit is the Lord Jesus Christ. The essence of Jesus is love, and the essence of the Holy Spirit is love. Therefore one of the most important roles associated with the Holy Spirit is love. Love then, is an additional foundation for the Gifts of the Spirit.

The fruit of the Spirit reveals the character of Jesus, and the first fruit listed is love. Without love, even the Gifts of the Spirit are empty. It is through the Holy Spirit that the love of God is shed abroad in our hearts. It is the Holy Spirit who reveals the love of God to us, and who enables us to reveal the love of God to others. Love is displayed by the manner in which we relate to others, the things that we do for others, and keep the words of Jesus.[39]

God is love. We are to love Him and Jesus Christ with all of our being in every possible way and love others the same way we love ourselves. These are the *commandants* of Jesus Christ to us. It is *error* and *ungodly* not to love people of every type, race, language, and nationality. However, do not be deceived about love. Love is not a weakness. Nor is it a substitute for the wrath and hatred we should have against evil acts and satanic perversion of everything God has created for good.

Spiritually, non Believers *are* no different than *we were*.[40] The love of God is so great that He offered up Jesus Christ *for all*. We have eternal life because of God's love. Faith works by love. Love is better than all of the Gifts of the Holy Spirit combined. In fact, the Gifts of the Spirit are of little value if the person through whom they operate does not demonstrate love. Love and the Gifts of the Spirit are inseparable.[41] The next foundation is the Word of God.

Make God's Word Final Authority

Everything we learn about the Holy Spirit, His Gifts, and His power must be established upon the foundation of the Word of God, and the Word of God *must* be our final authority. *Opinion* is one thing, but facts from the written Word of God are irrefutable. *The Word of God must be the final authority* for what we know about God, the Lord Jesus Christ, the Holy Spirit and His Power, the Gifts of the Spirit, things pertaining to the Kingdom of God, and our conduct. *The Holy Spirit and His Gifts are inseparable from God's Word.*[42] However, we cannot make God's Word final authority if we do not *know* God's Word. Therefore, there is an activity associated with this foundation: *we must study God's Word.*

We only know what we have been taught. There is so very much *that we don't know*! We must study the scriptures so that we can be workmen approved of God, and with the help of the Holy Spirit, correctly understand the Word. Always ask the Holy Spirit for help to understand the scriptures.

Study the Word of God

Only the Word of God gives knowledge, instruction, and information about all things that pertain to life and Godliness, and all of the promises of God. All of the promises of God are yes and so be it, in Christ Jesus. The Holy Spirit, His Gifts, and His power is a *major promise* of God for those that belong to the Lord Jesus Christ. The *supporting scriptures* in this book are directly or indirectly related to the subjects that are presented. Study these scriptures carefully and read them to yourself *out loud* along with other scriptures from the Word of God that are related to the Holy Spirit.

By doing this you will increase your faith and desire to have the Holy Spirit, His Gifts, and His power to operate through you. This is because faith comes by continually hearing the Word of God. When you hear what you are reading out loud about receiving the promise of the Holy Spirit and His Gifts, your faith will grow and increase, and your desire will become strong to have them. Once you desire and crave to have the Gifts of the Holy Spirit operate through you, pray to receive this mighty blessing. Having done this, there are certain *activities* in which we need to engage.

The Activity of Prayer

Prayer is direct connection to God and communication with Him. Jesus tells us that men ought to always pray. Helping us to pray is an essential role of the Holy Spirit. The Word of God tells us to pray always with *all kinds* of prayer in the Spirit. In addition, it is the Holy Spirit who enables us to build up ourselves on our most holy faith. Since the connection between the Holy Spirit and prayer is so interrelated, let's take a closer look at this activity.[43]

If you were to carefully study both the Old Testament and the New Testament, you will find that the greatest encounter people had with God came *while in prayer* or *after* prayer. I have found this to be especially true during worship; which is prayer that maintains a relationship of love for God and fellowship with Him. Jesus, Peter, and Paul were like praying machines. We should be likewise. The Gifts of the Spirit are very often manifested during times of prayer. Pray to exercise love. Pray *to know* the Holy Spirit; it's of little value to just know *about* Him. Desire and pray for the Gifts of the Spirit to operate through *you* as the Holy Spirit wills. Jesus clearly revealed the attitude of God in giving the Holy Spirit to those who ask.[44] We have not because we ask not. We ask through prayer. Pray and ask! In this chapter you will find *how* to pray several *essential* prayers.

It is meaningful for us to understand that when we pray God hears us; especially when we pray in the Name of Jesus Christ and according to His will, which is His Word.[45] Now, to be told that God will hear you when you pray is a pretty bold statement to make. I will prove to you from scripture and by a clear cut example of something which occurred in my own life, that this is true. Here are some examples from scripture.

In the Old Testament, Daniel had a vision that he didn't understand. So he prayed. Now get this! *While he was praying*, God sent an angel to give Daniel understanding of that vision. Furthermore, the angel stated that he was dispatched by God to bring the answer *at the beginning* of Daniel's prayer. God heard Daniel's prayer, and He will hear ours.[46]

In the New Testament Early Church, a Roman centurion named Cornelius, *who was not a Christian* but loved God, prayed always and had fasted for four days. God heard *his* prayers and sent an angel to him with instructions as to what he should do to receive eternal salvation, the Holy Spirit, and be baptized into the Body of Christ.[47] If God heard Cornelius' prayers, He certainly will hear yours if you belong to the Lord Jesus Christ.

The Holy Spirit Reveals God through Prayer

Here's something else that is good for us to realize. God *wants us* to know Him, and He has *made provisions* for us *to know* Him. First, He sent Jesus Christ, who is the express image of His person, to reveal Him. To know Jesus is to know God. Then, God sent the Holy Spirit so that Jesus could be revealed to us *now*. The Holy Spirit reveals Jesus to us *directly, and also through the Word of God*.[48]

But there is a role *we* must play. His Word says that *if* we seek for Him with all of our heart, we will find Him. In other words, God *will* be *revealed* to us, *if we really seek Him*. To reveal means to disclose, uncover, expose, and make evident that which was hidden. We're talking about God! I personally know for a fact that seeking Him diligently brings rewards and causes Him to be revealed to us. But it's not an overnight exercise. It takes sincere, heart serious prayer *over a sustained period of time* to really get to know Him. Given the times in which we are living, and the nature of the times to come, *it is vital that we know Him!*[49]

The Holy Spirit, Revelation of God's Word, Prayer

When you meditate on God's Word with prayer, the Holy Spirit will often give you a revelation that has a profound impact on you because of the Divine disclosure of the meaning of that scripture. You literally see what the scripture means from God's point of view, and it is usually *verified by other supporting scriptures*. Let me give you an example.

A number of years ago before becoming a minister, I was in sustained prayer when the Holy Spirit spoke these words to me: "In Him dwelleth all the fullness of the Godhead bodily and you are complete in Him." I went to a pastor to find out what that meant. His response was, "What does it mean *to you?*" I didn't know, but I kept that scripture in my heart for years.

Years later, as I was in prayer, the Holy Spirit reminded me of that scripture again. *Then* He gave me an astounding revelation of it. I believe this revelation was reserved for me because of the times in which we are living, and the character of the times to come. This revelation will have an awesome impact on the prayer life of anyone who believes it and receives it as I did.

Here's the revelation and amazing significance of this scripture: *everything* God the Father and God the

Holy Spirit is, dwells in the Lord Jesus Christ *bodily*. And if we belong to Jesus Christ, then *everything* God the Father, the Holy Spirit, and the Lord Jesus Christ is, dwells in us *spiritually*. The reason we are complete in Jesus Christ is because *through Him*, all of the members of Godhead dwell *in us spiritually*. They dwell in us as the Spirit of the Lord, as the Holy Spirit Himself, and as the Spirit of Christ. This is why we are complete in Him. Awesome!

Scripture says that we are the *Body* of Christ, and He is our *Head*. Hence, we are united together. He is seated at the Right Hand of God in Heaven. And, we are seated in Heavenly places in Him. All power in Heaven and Earth is given to Him in whom dwells all of the fullness of the Godhead bodily, and we are complete in Him. Remember, He is *in us*, and we are *in Him*. Therefore, *as He is, so are we* in *this* world![50] However, *we are not* and *we shall never be* Divine like *He is, and as He shall forever be*. But because we are His Body, we have the blessed ability to draw upon *His* Divine resources.

A total belief and understanding of these facts can give us a whole new perspective of Heaven's view of us, the overwhelming authority and power we have, and how we can see things as though looking down from on High through the eyes of Jesus Christ. Meditate on this!

Personal Proof that Prayer Works

Now here is the personal example I promised to share with you that God hears our prayers. It also shows how the Gifts of the Spirit can be associated with prayer, and how they can manifest outside of a church service environment.

The ultimate confirmation that God hears our prayers

occurred to me about nine months before my first public ministry experience. Near our home was a high school with a beautiful, peaceful campus where I would daily spend hours praying. On one occasion, I naïvely and vociferously complained to the Lord about the lack of ministry opportunities. Little did I realize that the hours upon hours of prayer and studying of the Word was His method of *first* preparing me for what He had called me to do. I presented Him with concerns that *I felt were major*; all of which were wrapped in disappointment and frustration. Now comes the most astounding part of all.

When I returned home, my wife informed me that we were invited to dinner by a minister we knew and loved dearly. At various times in her life all nine Gifts of the Holy Spirit flowed through her. We went to her home for dinner that evening. Amazingly, proof that God hears prayer was demonstrated to me at that time by the Gifts of the Holy Spirit, *that manifested through her*. This is a prime example of the Holy Spirit knowing about our prayers, and bringing a response to them *from* the Lord Jesus Christ Himself. Here's what happened.

After asking me to bless the food, the Gifts of the Spirit manifested through this marvelous saint and she began to prophesy. In her prophesying, the Word of Knowledge and the Word of Wisdom came forth. She pointed her finger at me, and by the Spirit *she repeated the exact things I had said to the Lord four hours earlier*. She then gave the Lord's reply to my concerns; which included tremendous exhortation and comfort. There was absolutely no way that she could possibly have known *what I had said to the Lord in prayer earlier that day!* But Jesus knew, and the Holy Spirit gave me the Lord's answer through her. Be assured, God hears our prayers!

Thanksgiving, Praise, and Worship

There are *many* types of prayer. There are prayers of petition, intercession, thanksgiving, praise, worship, and many more. All of these have their place. Prayers of petition are probably used more than any other type of prayer. This is the type of prayer where God is always being asked to do something in response to some type of need or desire. Usually it involves, "God I need you to give me something." Please don't misunderstand me. There are times when this type of prayer is needed and appropriate. But not *all* the time! God knows *everything*; including what we have need of. But He clearly tells us to seek first the Kingdom of God and His righteousness, and all *the things* we have need of will be added to us.

My personal priority of prayer is thanksgiving for the wonderful things He has already done, followed by praise because of His greatness and majesty, followed by worship; because worship involves a personal, intimate relationship of adoration, love, and fellowship with God.

Continually thank God for His love, for Jesus Christ, for the Holy Spirit, for progressively giving you understanding of the Kingdom of God and His righteousness, and for giving you favor to be used by the Holy Spirit and His Gifts. Praise God because He is great and marvelous. We *demonstrate* praise when *we tell Him* about the great and mighty things He has done, *and is doing*. Worship Him because you love Him. As demonstrated by others throughout scripture, I too have found that the Gifts of the Spirit manifest very often during times of prayer. You may also be surprised to find that a life style of worship decreases the need for prayers of petition.

Love plus Prayer is Powerful

I have mentioned love and prayer. The Holy Spirit has just brought something to my attention related to love and prayer that I believe He wants me to share with you.

Although I had received Jesus Christ as my personal Savior at the age of twelve, twenty-five years later as a professor at a medical center in New York, I began to seriously drift away from the things of God

One weekend, my family and I dropped by to see my best friend from childhood. We both, at the same church service, received Jesus Christ as our personal Savior in a little one-room Baptist church in rural Virginia. To this day, there has never been a time when we didn't know and love one another like the closest of brothers. While visiting on *this* particular occasion, the subject of Jesus Christ came up. I proceeded to give my *new founded philosophy* about Jesus. My friend looked at me with disbelief and said, "Are you saved?" My answer was, "Of course I'm saved." He said, "How do you know?" My answer, "Because *I feel* saved." Wrong! His wife simply looked at me and while gently shaking her head and smiling said, "I'm going to pray for you." Well, you can probably tell from reading this book, that this wonderful lady's prayers are pretty effective.

But here's the point. Although these people really love God *and also know* unscriptural spiritual nonsense when they hear it, their love for me never changed. They simply prayed and God responded. The bottom line is this: love and prayer together is a very powerful combination!

The author believes the following prayers to be *absolutely essential* for Believers:

Pray to Know the Love of Christ

"Father in the Name of Jesus I pray that Christ may dwell in my heart by faith, and that I being rooted and grounded in love, may be able to comprehend with all saints what is the breadth, and length, and depth, and height; and to know the love of Christ, which passes knowledge, that I may be filled with all the fullness of God."[51]

Pray to Know the Greatness of the Holy Spirit

"Father in the Name of the Lord Jesus, I pray that I might know the exceeding greatness of the power of the Holy Spirit which You wrought in Christ when You raised Him from the dead and set Him at your own right hand in heavenly places."[52]

Pray to Receive the Gifts of the Holy Spirit

"Father, according to your Word, I desire to have the Gifts of the Holy Spirit operate in my life according to His will that through me the Lord Jesus Christ may be revealed and glorified, that through me Your Kingdom may be demonstrated, and that I may be a blessing to others.

In the Name of Jesus Christ I pray. Amen"

Except for Prophecy, the Word of God *does not* tell us *which* Gifts of the Spirit to desire. But you will find that *the Gifts you desire* are in line with the work or ministry God desires for you to do. Once a Gift is given to operate through you it is never recalled.[53] The Gift is always available for the Holy Spirit to operate through you as He wills.

The Activity of Faith

Faith without works is dead.[54] Once you believe something in God's Word, or something that the Holy Spirit has revealed to you related to God's Word, act on it! A good place to start is with the Inward Witness. Now that you know that the Holy Spirit leads by the Inward Witness, the next time you lose something ask the Holy Spirit to help you to find it! The first few times you do this may not seem to work. Just keep on! The Holy Spirit will see that you *are persistently* trusting and relying upon *Him.* The more you trust Him, the more *He begins to trust you* and will then lead you into *greater* things.

Let me share a few words with you about faith that you may find interesting. Without faith we cannot please God. But since you have been given the measure of faith by Him, *you have* faith. The main thing then, is how well your faith can be increased and developed. One of the best ways to increase faith is to read the scriptures *out loud.* When doing this we hear what we are reading. Remember, *faith comes by hearing* the Word of God. Then, we develop our faith by *believing* and *doing* what we've *heard* and *read* from the Word. Praying in the Spirit also helps us *to build up* our faith.[55] Never feel put down because your faith is not at the level of someone else's. Just keep on increasing and developing *your* faith.

Position Yourself to be used by the Holy Spirit

Let me recommend some additional things you may wish to consider to place yourself into position to be more greatly used by the Holy Spirit *and* His Spiritual Gifts. Passionately desire the Gifts of the Holy Spirit. Pray diligently and sincerely for them. Have the right motives, and purpose to develop a Christ-like life and corresponding ministry. You may be thinking to yourself, me! A minister? Yes, *you!* Here's why.

All who belong to Christ are ambassadors for Him, for the Kingdom of God, and have been automatically given a ministry called "The ministry of reconciliation."[56] This has nothing to do with being, "Called into *the* ministry," as a Five Fold Ministry Gift. The ministry of reconciliation is the ministry of letting *all* people know about the love of God, and what His Son the Lord Jesus Christ has *done for them,* and what is *now available to them* because of the death, burial, and resurrection of Jesus.

Because of sin man was separated from God. Since he was separated from God, man couldn't know God. Since he couldn't know God, man couldn't be like God. Jesus fixed all of that through His earthly ministry, and His death, burial, and resurrection. The ministry of reconciliation is to let *all* people know that their sins and transgressions against God *have already been forgiven* and that they can be reconciled to God simply by receiving the Lord Jesus Christ as their personal Savior. By the way, this word *reconciliation* has an awesome meaning. It means to heal, harmonize, and restore divine favor. This is what Jesus has done for us *with God!*

The ministry of reconciliation is one that all Believers *are supposed* to engage in. By doing so, *you* are engaged in the most important of *all* ministries. This has *nothing* to do with *religion*. It has *everything* to do with *relationship*: Relationship between God and people. Because of His love for all people that He created, and His desire for them to be saved, God has every incentive to help us. **Therefore, He has sent and made available to us the Holy Spirit with His Gifts to help us in this most important of all ministries.**

Along with this ministry, we should desire to develop a Christ-like life. This is a life patterned after the love and character of Jesus. This involves a process and takes time. As we yield ourselves to the Lord with all of our heart and strive to live a life of love, righteousness, and domination over evil, the Holy Spirit works to perfect us in these areas. This *does not* mean we are to go off into seclusion and completely disassociate ourselves from family, friends, and people, or project an air of being more holy than everybody else. Jesus *is not,* and *never was* like that! We should, however, strive to live our lives according to the commandments and dictates of scripture.

With the help of the Holy Spirit, Jesus glorified and revealed the nature and character of God, demonstrated the Kingdom of God, was a blessing to people, and reconciled people to God. We should strive to do likewise.

Move Up Higher in God

By now you know that the marvelous supernatural Gifts of the Holy Spirit are manifested by the Spirit as He wills. You also know that God is no respecter of persons. This means that you are a candidate for the Gifts to operate through you if it is your desire and if you have the right motives.

The Holy Spirit is sensitive and very gentle. The more sensitive *we are* to the needs of others and the love of God, the better. The Holy Spirit is pure, holy, and good. He wants to use us, but He will never impose Himself upon us. We have *to desire* to be used by Him and we have to ask Him to use us. Let's *be willing* to allow Him to perfect that which concerns us for His use.

Follow love, and *desire* spiritual Gifts, *just as scripture tells us to do!* [57] The best way to demonstrate your desire and willingness to be used by Him is to pray. Through relentless and sincere prayers of worship and adoration, crave *and ask* the Holy Spirit to mold and fashion you with the qualities He wants you to have for His magnificent Gifts to flow through you. *He wants you to move up higher in God.* His response to your persistent adoration of Him and desire to be used by Him will amaze you. What a blessing *you and the Holy Spirit* are going to be to others!

Supporting Scriptures:
Essential Steps to Take
Please read the scriptures

---

[1] 2Cor11:3
[2] Jn14:6, Acts 2:22-24, Heb1:1-3, 2Ti 4:1
[3] 1Cor 15:3,4
[4] Jas 5:14, 15

[5] Acts 1:5, Lk 11:13. Mt 6:33

Baptism with the Holy Spirit
[6] Jn 16:12,13, 1 Cor 3:2
[7] Is 28:9,10
[8] Acts 1:2,4-5,8-9, Jn 14:15
[9] Mt 28:18-20
[10] Mt 28:18-20, Mk 16:15-20, Lk 24:49
[11] Acts 1:2-5, 2:4, 17, 18, 38, 39, 10:42-46, 19:2-6
[12] Eph 2:10, 1 Cor3:9, Mk 16:20, Heb 2:3,4
[13] 1 Cor 2:4, Acts 10:44-46, Rom 15:19, Lk 24:49
[14] Acts 2:3,4, 10:44-46, Is 28:11, 1 Cor14:21, Mt 3:11, Mk 16:16,17, Acts 2:38,39
[15] Lk11:9,10,13
[16] Acts 19:1-7
[17] Matt 3:11, Jn7:38-39, Mk16:16-17

Tongues
[18] Mk 16:16,17, Acts 2:3,4, Acts 10:44-47, Acts 19:1-6
[19] Acts 2:4,11, 1Cor 14:12-15, 13:1
[20] 1 Cor12:10
[21] 1 Cor12:28
[22] 1 Cor14:5
[23] Rom 8:26, 27
[24] 1 Cor 14:14, 15
[25] 1 Cor 14:18, 39
[26] 2 Ti 3:16, 2 Cor 1:3, Jn 14:28, 16:13

2 Kingdoms
[27] Eph 3:14, 15
[28] Jn 17:20-23, Lk 17:21
[29] Rom 14:17
[30] Mt 12:28, 8:16, Lk 8:24,25, Jn 12:17, Lk 7:11-15, Mt 4:23, Mt 17:24-27, Mk 6:35-42, Jn 2:1-10
[31] Jn 14:12, Acts 1:8, Mk 16:15-20
[32] Lk 12:32, Dan 7:27, Dan 4:3
[33] Ps 145:13
[34] Rev 16:10, 20:10

[35] Col 1:12, 13
[36] Jas 2:19, 2, Mk 1:23,24, 1 Cor 4:3,4,
[37] 2 Cor 10:4, Phil 2:9, 10, Rev 12:11, Mt 4:4,7,10
[38] Mt 16:16-19
[39] Rom 5:5, Jn 15:17, 14:23

Love
[40] Eph 2:1-13
[41] Gal 5:22, 1 Jn 4:8, Mt 22:37-39, Jn 3:16, Gal 5:6, 1 Cor 12:31, 13:1
[42] 2 Ti 3:15, Rom 10:17

Prayer
[43] Lk 18:1, Eph 6:18, Jude 20
[44] Lk 11:13,
[45] Jn 14:14, 1 Jn 5:14,
[46] Dan 10:2, 3, 12., Jer 33:3
[47] Acts 10:1-48
[48] Jer 29:13, Jn 14:8,9, Heb 1:3, Jn 14:6, 16:13
[49] 2 Ti 3:1, 2 Pet 3:9
[50] 1 Cor 12:27, Col 1:18, Jn 17:23, Heb 12:2, Eph 2:6, Col 2:9,10, 1 Jn 4:17
[51] Eph 3:14-19
[52] Eph 1:17-22
[53] Rom 11:29
[54] Jas 2:20
[55] Heb 11:6, Rom 12:3
[56] 2 Cor 5:18-21
[57] 1 Cor 14:1

CONCLUDING REMARKS

God existed *before* eternity past and shall exist throughout eternity future. He is the only One who has told from the beginning what the end will be for mankind.[1] Common sense tells us that if everything God has predicted through the Word of God from the Book of Genesis up until this present time has come to pass, exactly as it was foretold, then everything from here on out will also come to pass exactly as He has indicted that it will. We are living during a critical time period where Biblical prophecy and earthly historical events have merged, and soon a *new time period* for mankind will be ushered in.

The state and condition of our eternal being and existence will be determined by what we do, or fail to do, now. The Holy Spirit, His Gifts, and His Power are *critical* at this particular time in history and *vital* to us at this particular time in our lives. The most important things anyone can do in *this life now* are to receive the Lord Jesus Christ as their personal Savior and be baptized with the Holy Spirit. The only true safety we have is in the Lord.[2] This the unbeliever does not believe, and the ignorant does not know. But *you now know!* That's why this book has been written, and that is why the essence of this paragraph which has been stated before, has been stated again.

The Holy Spirit and His Gifts *are for You*

It is my deepest desire that you have found information, insight, and inspiration from this book and that it has been of enormous value to you. To have the supernatural Gifts and Power of the Holy Spirit *regularly* operate through you, *delight* yourself in the Lord, *desire* them, and *want* them. As you study *the supporting scriptures* that have been listed, and other *related scriptures*, pray and desire to be used by the Holy Spirit with His Gifts operating through *you*.

The biggest mistake some people make is to feel that they are unworthy, unqualified, untrained, must be a Minister of the Gospel, or, that the Holy Spirit will use others, *but not them*! This is not true! Listen, for those He chooses to use, God does not confine Himself to *man-made* selections based upon *man-made* requirements and credentials. Before coming to Jesus, the Apostle Paul was personally trained by one of the most brilliant scholars of all times. Before coming to Jesus, the Apostle Peter was a simple, uneducated, fisherman. Yet, God used both of them mightily. God has *His own standards* and He looks at your heart! In fact, being with Jesus compensates for all man-made inadequacies. Believe me, He can use *you* too![3] Read Acts Chapter 4, verse thirteen to verse sixteen, *and think about it!* Now let's look at scriptural proof showing that the Holy Spirit will use a "regular" Believer. Then we'll follow up with a "modern day" example.

In the Book of the Acts there was a "certain disciple" named Ananias that had a vision. In this vision he heard the voice of the Lord telling him to go to a particular house where a previously dangerous man, who persecuted Believers even to the point of death, named Saul was praying. In addition, the Lord told Ananias that Saul, who later became the Apostle Paul, was praying and that while praying, *he also* had a vision. In *his vision*, Saul saw Ananias coming and laying hands upon him so he could receive his sight. Saul became blind as he was on his way to persecute some Believers and had an encounter with the Lord Jesus Christ. Ananias wasn't too enthused about this assignment. But after receiving more information, he followed the Lord's instructions and Saul received his sight.

Here's what I believe the Holy Spirit really wants *us to see*. Ananias was merely a "certain disciple". In other words, *he was a regular Believer*. Yet the Lord spoke to him, Gifts of the Spirit operated through Him, and the power of the Holy Spirit flowing through his hands enabled Saul, who was blind, to receive his sight. This is an example of the Holy Spirit, His Gifts, and His Power operating through a "regular" Believer in the Early Church regarding an extremely important event. The Holy Spirit has not changed. Now let's look at some of His activities through "regular" Believers during recent years.

A number of years ago a business woman who heard of our Ministry felt impressed that we should come to Atlanta, Georgia to minister. Being a devout Believer, she went into prayer and was later led by the Holy Spirit to discuss her ideas with several other Christian women. Through prayer and the leading of the Holy Spirit, this small group of about ten women contacted our Ministry to see if we would allow *them* to sponsor us for a Saturday one-night service in the Atlanta area. Feeling that this would be pleasing to the Lord, we agreed and they made all of the arrangements.

Several months later, upon our arrival at the airport in Atlanta, we were warmly met by a delegation of four women: the business woman, and three other women who had not known or seen me before. Now we will see the main thing that I believe the Holy Spirit wants to be emphasized.

As I went to greet the three other women, one of them stepped back, put her hands up to her mouth, and said in a manner that seemed to amaze her, "You are *the exact same man I saw getting off of the airplane* while I was praying! You are even dressed in the same clothes!" None of these women were ministers. As "regular" Believers they were all doing what they believed the Lord wanted to be done. What this woman saw in a vision given to her by the Holy Spirit, was a Word of Wisdom that came to pass as it was previously revealed to her in that vision. My appearance, as she saw it in the vision, was confirmation to them that what they were doing was surely approved of God. The meeting, held in a large hotel room, I believe was a success in the eyes of God and man. The people were blessed, and I was glad that we all obeyed the leading of the Holy Spirit.

Let this example be a confirmation *to you* that the Lord is no respecter of persons and will use you too. Regardless of whom you are, the Holy Spirit wants to lead you, guide you, and have His Gifts and Power flow *through you* as well as through *anybody* else!

May the Lord Jesus Christ richly bless you, keep you in the truth of His Word, use you to glorify Him by the Holy Spirit, and enable you by the Holy Spirit to bring others to the Lord Jesus Christ for eternal salvation and kingship under God.[4]

To Ministers of the Gospel of Jesus Christ

To be called to minister the Gospel of the Lord Jesus Christ is, in my opinion, the highest and greatest of all human endeavors. It also carries the greatest of all responsibilities. Just as the nation of Israel and its people were the oracles and chosen representatives of God during the Old Testament times, the Lord has chosen the Body of Christ to be His representatives during this dispensation of Grace. To fulfill this role He has given the Body of Christ three precious gifts: The Word of God, The Holy Spirit with His Gifts and Power, and The Five Fold Ministry Gifts that stand in the offices of the apostles, prophets, evangelists, pastors and teachers. As such, *you* are a very precious Gift!

The Holy Spirit is given to help and benefit all Believers. Likewise, He is given to help and benefit all of those who are called to any of the Five Fold Ministry offices.

Fulfilling the commandments of Jesus will lead us to embrace the Holy Spirit, His Power, His Gifts, and enable us to more strikingly demonstrate the Kingdom of God. When we do this, the more God the Father and the Lord Jesus Christ are glorified by the Holy Spirit. The more Jesus is glorified, the more unbelievers will receive Him as their personal Savior. This is *the work of God:* to get people to believe on Jesus Christ whom God has sent. Those who do *this work* are wise and shall shine as stars forever. This is part of the Great Commission, and it is the essential *work of the ministry* that *we in the Five Fold Ministry* are responsible to do and teach. But this work cannot be done without the fullness of the Holy Spirit.[5]

Any church representing the Lord Jesus Christ can have a dignified and beautiful liturgical worship service and yet demonstrate the glory of God through the Gifts and Power of the Holy Spirit. It's all a matter of knowledge and obedience to the Word of God.

I trust this book has been a blessing to you. My sincere desire is that the Lord richly blesses you, the ministry He has entrusted to you, and that through a Christ-like life and ministry, you will be an even greater blessing to Believers, the Body of Christ, and to others.

Supporting Scriptures:
Concluding Remarks
Please read the scriptures

---

[1] 1 Ti 1:17, Isa 46:10
[2] Psm 34:7,6,4, Psm 4:8
[3] Acts 22:3, 5:34, Mk 1:16, Acts 4:13
[4] Rev 1:5,6
[5] Jn 6:28,29, Prov 11:30, Dan 12:2,3, Mk 16:15-20

A PRAYER OF BLESSINGS

May the Most High God, the Almighty One, the Eternal One, the God of Love and Peace, the God of Abraham, Isaac, and Jacob, and God the Father of the Lord Jesus Christ command these blessings upon you.

Be blessed to receive and love the Lord Jesus Christ and Almighty God with all of your heart, soul, mind, and strength. Be blessed to know the love of the Lord Jesus Christ which passes all understanding. Be blessed to know the Holy Spirit and His Power which raised Jesus Christ from the dead. Be showered with His mercy and grace. Be strengthened with His might and ability. May you be blessed by the Spirit of Glory to bring glory, and honor, and praise to the Lord Jesus Christ. Be blessed spiritually, mentally, and physically. Be blessed financially, and in your relationships.

May you and your entire household be eternally kept in the Kingdom of God by His Word and Divine Power. May the angels of the Most High take charge over you and yours to keep you from all hurt, harm, and dangers; seen and unseen. With long life may you be satisfied.

May the grace of the Lord Jesus Christ, the love of God, and the communion of the Holy Spirit, be with you always. In the Name Jesus Christ I pray. Amen.

Eugene G. Givens, DDS

Special Statement

It is the Lord Jesus Christ who deserves all the glory, honor, praise, and thanksgiving for any blessing anyone receives from this book.

Special Request

Please let the Holy Spirit use you to spread the message and information in this book to others through "word of mouth," emails, Face Book, Twitter and other forms of social networking, and by referring them to
Books of Value
at
www.booksofvalue.com